I0468821

The Winning Habit: **Recipes for corporate renewal.**

Introduction:

Since writing this original thesis the world has changed at alarming pace. We are now in a world recession that is in my mind partly due to over gearing of corporate buy-outs, and the suppression of organic creativity. Banks have lent to corporations not on commercial principals but largely joined the hysterical money grab mentality of false corporate growth through shear financial gearing momentum. Harm has obviously been to done to everything from pensions to international aid programmes. One of the greatest injuries of this last cycle has been the near expunging of creativity, which should, if economies are to grow, be a major force for sound organic growth.

This handbook is about the management of conflicting forces; to ensure the survival of individual enterprises, no matter what their size. Each 'body corporate' has to obey the same rules to survive and to grow.

The management of opposites is the unavoidable puzzle that has to be solved..

'Opposite' means what it says, e.g. order versus disorder, organised systems versus creative flair, efficient administrators versus inspirational entrepreneurs, methodical analysis versus hypothetical theory. Most of all it means our ability; to learn from history, but not to be imprisoned by it, and also to have the courage to build a future in the realms of the unknown and untried.

The balance of effective administration of the present and creative innovation for the future is enormously difficult to bring off. Leaders with the qualities to deliver this equation are few and far between.

The reasons are manifold, from education to the culture of business and tribal law. After all people who get to the top get there by being; crafty, politically astute, but most of all successful. The record of success is probably the biggest single factor that inhibits long-term success. If we've been successful then it's natural to try to repeat the formula and keep trying it, until it's too late and it fails.

Over the last thirty years there have been numerous tomes written about the latest idea to ensure corporate success, in response to which an almost endless line of new 'business gurus' have trumpeted new formulae. Nevertheless business failures continue. In general take-overs and mergers are generally unimaginative defences; often the taken over enterprise is wasted and swallowed into a corporate oblivion, where identity and ideas are lost forever. How many companies and ideas of value have been smothered? Even in the twenty-first century, in an age of perceived creative innovation, corporate predation lays waste to more good ideas than it generates.

1

We have to face the fact that most corporations have a paucity of new ideas. Their founding idea, their original raison d'etre is usually the only one that has ever been a fountainhead of growth. Thereafter begins a war for market share, a defence against the competition and the gradual sinking from the entrepreneurial beginning to an often turgid death by takeover or insolvency.

Time is the measure of success, to be successful over two years is one thing, two hundred is quite another; and much rarer. (Outside those great Chemical giants such as ICI, Nobel, Bayer et al there are fewer examples of truly creative international corporations. Even the oldest auto maker still makes cars. Money lenders, Bankers, who live off other people's ideas, whilst the great land owning dynasties with mineral rights such as Oil companies are the most common old timers. (They of course are innovative engineers but their one idea is to exploit natural fuel reserves. who would have thought that fossil fuels - coal and oil would be so under pressure from environmentalists and global warming, just ten years ago?.)

I could have called this book; 'How to have new ideas, build on them and then have some more.' That surely would have been a bit cumbersome. Only a handful of companies ever use constant innovation as a primary strategy. The purpose of this book is to help the reader to harness this elusive concept.

The book is written in three sections, **Part 1** "It's the People that count."
Part 2, "Improving day by day." and   **Part 3** "Creating a future."

The **Part 1** deals with the basic systems of day to day running of the enterprise. The emphasis lies in its basic premise, that it is the team that has to work the systems, which aren't worth a lickety-spit if you have the wrong talents in the wrong jobs.

Effective improving systems will not work in rigid organisations. Flexible organisations are like, flexible gearboxes; where each individual is at THE centre, an indispensable cog. That individual's perception of the world is that he or she are at the centre of it, and it is from that standpoint that they see the organisation. Organisations need to reflect this.

Companies consist of more than just the leader, so Part 1 starts addressing the needs and compatibilities of those individuals who want to be part of the living enterprise. I call this the Body Corporate and I draw specific analogies with the human body. I talk of fitness, energy, brains, heart and muscle.

"It's the people that count." In Part 1 indicates ways of keeping the body corporate healthy and alive.

Part 2 deals with the processes of innovative thinking and the culture necessary to sustain it.   It addresses how continuous innovation supplants continuous improvement. it confirms that even the best performer that relies on the principles described in part 1 alone is doomed to an early end without the regenerative ability of innovation.

Part 3 points to ways of sustaining the corporation through time and how to move the horizons of aspiration forward continuously; "Creating one's own corporate future". **Part 3** suggests ways to seek constant rejuvenation of the body corporate.

Hand on Heart. At the end of each section in the Blue and Red Books there are a series of questions. If readers ask themselves these questions and answer them honestly, they will get full value from this work. Acting on these answers will improve the performance of organisations, their continuous improvement practices as well as their appreciation of creativity in action.

Part 3 encompasses the whole; examining the types of organisations that are most likely to succeed, the processes of team development and leadership cultures. There are answers here for those who recognise the dilemma of managing opposites, and there are pointers for those who think they've got it licked.

The finale balances these conflicting ambitions, which give if not everlasting corporate life; something a little nearer 200years than 2, for some at least. The summaries are written from a practical standpoint. This is not an academic tome; I hope it will be a practical handbook for aspiring managers and business leaders in the early twenty first century.

Part 1.

Survival and health

Chapter 1
Effectiveness

Section 1

Effective Teams:

We can't all be the boss, but we can all contribute to the effectiveness of the organisation to which we belong. A team of people, large or small, will only compete effectively if the sum of the parts produces goods or services that are uniquely different from its competitors.

To do this there needs to be order, efficiency and measurable differential performance against the market competition.

As teams are made up of individuals, it is crucial that the corporation identifies its human resource requirements to fit the goals and culture as well as to its functional needs.

Enterprises in defensive mode tend to focus on function, rather than on the culture profile. Companies in an aggressive and expanding mode tend to emphasise the culture profile to the detriment of functional excellence. There seems to be an inevitable style drift[1]. This is quite understandable; 'our sort of chap' versus 'we need to tighten up debtors' control' is a natural response to prevailing conditions. The snag with this style drift is that we get teams that are not easily moulded into a unity of purpose. The teams are teams no longer, as the culture style drifts, but a collection of groups or individuals with diverse and contrary goals.

Individual executives need to agree about what the team profile looks like. This is a complex process and goes far beyond the 'we employ bright people'. The Body Corporate needs Brains, it needs a Heart and it needs Muscle. Put another way; it needs thinkers and analysts, leaders and drivers. Most important however, is that these functions are integrated.

As individuals, each team member bears his or her responsibility for effective performance. No one can make you effective other than yourself. Half way through a career we have acquired a lot of habits; some good ones, but certainly some bad ones too. If we want to be a major contributor to the enterprise where we work then we have no choice other than to accept the responsibility for our actions. Perhaps reading this book will help.

This book therefore is for the individual. It's for you, it's about self-awareness and self-appreciation, and it's about your role at the centre of the organisation that is certainly a large part of your life.

This notion that every one sits at the centre of their universe is a simple one, and is such a self-evident truth that it is often ignored. The relatively modern hierarchical

---

[1] Patricia Wilson –Social Style flex as a management tool. 1997
Prof. Bill Redding Style drift vs Style flex - Iford International Institute 1972

structure though now much flattened, goes only a small way to recognising this certitude, 'I am at the centre of my world'.

How then does the so called modern body corporate function if it is to accommodate all these individual aspirations? Each one focused from his or her unique standpoint. The imperative must be to create a functional context where each and every individual fits. More than that, not only must every individual know where he or she fits, they must know what is expected of them, and the value of their contribution to the corporation.

The workers charter; from CEO to the humblest should hold good:. To whom am I responsible? What is the definition of my job? What are the limits of my responsibility? Am I fairly measured and rewarded? If everyone in the organisation cannot answer these questions then they are unlikely to be effective contributors. Despite the obviousness of this 'charter' even in the top corporations (there are of course exceptions) job descriptions, definitions of responsibility are rare, often confined to shop floor workers and lower management. (see figure 1: example sketch of Job description; minimum content)

Fig 1: Job description

Job Title: Vice President, Sales & Marketing.   **Reports to**: C.E.O.

Job Holder: Anthony James.   **Date**: 25 December 2000

Main Purpose of Job: Description in less than 50 words.

Dimension of Responsibility: Sales Budget $15mn.   Expenditure budget: $4.8mn

Main contacts; Internal: C.E.O., B.o.D. colleagues., 6 direct reports.
                      External: Major customers, PR advisors, Ad agencies, Shareholders and analysts.

Key Result Areas:	Standards of Performance:
1 Achieve Sales budgets	Monthly and annual reports
2 Create Sales and Mktg Strategy	Strategic plan approved by shareholders
3 Sustain Market share to planned levels.	Industry association statistics.
4 Ensure accurate sales forecasts	Quarterly review performance against forecast
5 Ensure good customer relations	Periodic attitude surveys
6 Control expenditure within budget	Monthly and annual reports
7 Ensure own reports morale and training	Performance figures and staff turnover.
8 Self development	Agree 10 days per annum devoted to development training.

Fig 1 is an example and a simple one at that; however it serves to illustrate that this jobholder ought to be pretty clear what is expected from him. This description paints a fairly clear picture of who the inner ring relations are, (see internal contacts fig 1). These people have to be aware of any changes of the issues affecting the jobholder. The V.P. production will be very keen to see that sales forecasts are accurate and the V.P. finance will be locked onto the budgetary implications. Indeed it would be desirable that each job holder should study and understand the job descriptions of those inner ring relationships.

Where these disciplines are exercised they are often merely token initiatives. The job description once drafted is put away and never seen again, perhaps occasionally at appraisal time. Inevitable change renders even the humblest job description short term. It is much more difficult at the most responsible levels where the more generic decisions and responsibilities are harder to define.

As important as individual self-awareness and self-assurance is, the imperative remains to ensure the body corporate is moving as a homogeneous whole. (This is the reason after all that we choose to work for who we do.) Each contributor must be made aware of his or her part in achieving a genuine and immediate unity of purpose in the whole organisation. It is not possible to achieve operational effectiveness with a deficient organisation. The greater the pragmatic drift in organisational culture the less likely is operational success.

Viewing each contributor as the centre of his own world transforms formal hierchical organisations into sensitive dynamic ones, where atomic (individual) centres of activity interact into a molecular and integrated unit. (See figure 2b.)

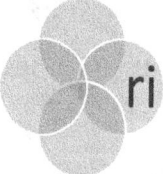

figure2a: Individually centred organisation. /b: Interactive inner ring relations.

The centre or nucleus is the jobholder and he or she relate to colleagues from this standpoint. The nucleus is valid for anyone CEO, sales person or factory supervisor. The outer rings are relative to the importance of colleague relationships. The CEO would see the inner conjunction as his Board colleagues, whereas the Sales person might see these close relationships with his territory manager and marketing support functions. These inner ring relationships are special and are built around the principle of mutual support. Thus rings of mutual support linking the whole organisation, are the primary channels for communication; particularly regarding issues of improved performance and support for corporate policy. These ring relationships can be formalised, or work on an informal basis.

Each job description must be seen and understood to network with those inner ring relationships, to recognise the boundaries, and impart a wider understanding of the outer ring relationships. From board strategy down to operative at whatever level, these individually centred jobs will relate dynamically to one another.

Groups of inner ring job relatives meet periodically to take note of changes and ensure up to date understanding of evolving strategies and imposed conditions. Changes are made by the related ring groups to reflect the new circumstances. Most obviously reviews are necessary in times that change from feast or famine, at new product introduction or in response to unplanned competitor intervention.

Thus the team members all feel they have a say in the management of their own jobs, and in the contribution to the business as a whole. This encourages thinking and learning, and opens up a dynamic dialogue at levels in the enterprise. It encourages teamwork and discourages isolationism and defensive reticence. It makes for a more effective team.

Hand on Heart:

- Do you and all those who report to you have up to date job descriptions?
- Do those job descriptions contain inner ring relationships references?
- Have you sat with inner ring relationships and discussed job interfaces?
- Do I and my fellows feel valued in this Corporation?
- Do we listen to and respect *all* our colleagues
- Do we listen to messages coming up as well as those coming down the command chain?

Section 2

Time, our most valuable resource.

In Section 1, I was at pains to point out that this book is for individuals who want to learn and contribute to the success of their enterprise whatever that might be. Most of us spend the majority of our lives asleep or at work. From our first job to our last, opportunity will pass by each minute. A minute well spent or a minute wasted?

I repeat, Time is the most precious resource we have. We have no choice other than to spend our allotted span. The question is do we spend it well? Sadly we cannot bank it, or save it, the instant between then and now is a constant moving untouchable portion out of our time ration. How can we spend it well?

The nature of time has been the focus of poets and philosophers; it ought to be the focus of more managers. In your career time or less glamorously, today's working time, it can be spent in and endless variety of ways. The issue in our context is, does the way we spend it advance the corporate cause or set it back?

Even the hardest working executive and the most extreme workaholic are inclined spend enormous amounts of time 'working', often ineffectually. We are frequently the only ones who can tell if our work is pertinent, and honestly applied. Is what we do necessary and the absolute priority? Or is it that we like doing best or is it the easiest work available out of a difficult range or is it the one with least risk attached or is it just to pass and kill time?

It would be ingenuous to expect maximum efficiency at all times, but would it be fair to take stock and re-examine how we spend our time? Habit and routine eat into our allotted span with a surprisingly consuming effect. Once more the enemy is, in a way, past experience. The calendar itself, morning prayers, weekly schedules, monthly meetings, reporting periods, annual meetings, all impose a strangling routine that almost enforces cataleptic habit. Far better, instead of calling meetings, we call for solutions or actions. What a difference that would make. If all the meetings resulted in actions that advanced the corporate cause, there would be far fewer called. What time would be liberated? Of course we have to have meetings but honesty states that we do not need as many.

The social culture of the corporation demands meetings. Often it would be more effective and time efficient if individuals; networking with their inner and outer ring colleagues handled problems more informally

Even if we are forced to attend meetings that consume an inordinate amount of our precious time, we would do well to review the way we spend our time, say on a fifteen-minute basis, at least twice a year. We will find that a far too small proportion of our working time is spent on the Key Result Areas of our jobs. An improvement of say a 5% of use of time across the organisation would yield a disproportionate benefit to overall performance.

If managers spent time visiting their reports rather than asking everyone to come to meetings with them, then time would be saved, the manager would see his supporting staff in their own environment and learn more of their problems and challenges. Sir John Harvey Jones the legendary leader of ICI in its hay day, always spent time as he called it; "just sitting on the desks of my colleagues and learning what they were about and how we could help each other"[2].(His key result Area – Leadership.) It saved time and it reinforced the bonds on inner ring relationships and negated the need for so many meetings.

In our individually centred organisation this issue of time management always remains a key task for continuous improvement. At worst saving time wasted on useless pursuits will improve morale, even if the time saved is spent on hygiene factors rather than Key Result Areas. Time therefore can be neutrally wasted, just idled away. Even worse it can be wasted negatively in the pursuit of the useless. It can be used optimally in the furtherance of Key Result Areas and it can be used well in improving both social and functional support structures.

Eliminating the wasted moment is a discipline crucial to effective individual performance.

Hand on Heart:

- Do we review job descriptions and Key Result Areas regularly?
- Can we cut the number of routine meetings?
- Do I review my activity diary at least once a quarter?
- Do I review my priorities regularly (weekly, monthly)?

---

[2] Sir John Harvey Jones – Making it happen – Profile Books

Section 3

The thinking contributors.

The brains of the business, of the body corporate are seen to be naturally vested in the leadership of the enterprise. Yet throughout all the corporations I have worked with I have found without exception that there is a huge reservoir of ability that lies largely untapped, not so much suppressed as ignored.

The system of conscious or unconscious hierarchy and the experience of it lead most of us to an almost unconscious arrogance that leadership bestows; infallibility and an unassailable self-reliance. We've come so far; surely our progress is not founded on the intellectual equivalent of 'fool's gold'? Experience must count for something? Surely it does, but it cannot replicate the innocently uncluttered thought processes of the younger and untainted enthusiast.

The liberation of talent is the single most important managerial role[3]. Once freed talent must be constructively channelled, a challenge that is much more positive than the policy of containment. So in addition to the formality of the job description this implies a 'what else' dimension, a dynamic that puts more than regimented discipline into the lives of the aspiring executive.

This is not a question of degree. Once talent is out of the bag, you cannot hope to restrain the protagonist without seriously demotivating him or her. The failure to have the courage to channel talent is amongst the chief reasons for staff wastage and the destructive lowering of morale. This is a life threatening disease that chokes the life out of many promising companies where the founders and bosses simply cannot let go. Many exciting start-ups fail to make the transition from their entrepreneurial beginnings to corporations of substance because the founders are afraid to liberate the talent that exists within their team. This disease is not confined to smaller companies. Many of those former market leaders who are swallowed up in destructive takeovers get what they deserve. The Management has atrophied, ignoring the bank of talent that if allowed, would have wrought change and breathed new life into the business.

'Vision' is much vaunted as the quality most desirable for a successful business leader. There's little wrong with the assertion, except perhaps that it implies that vision is confined to the very top of the organisation. Why? Surely it is equally valid and just as relevant that a production foreman can have a vision for the better running of his section, or the service he receives, or the quality aspirations of his department.

This is a good example of our 'Individually centred organisation' it is almost certain that the production foreman will have a 'vision' of what his department can deliver and how it can be improved. This 'vision' may not be as grand as matters of globalisation, or market share domination, but nevertheless it is a profoundly

---

[3] Gary Hamel - Leading the revolution —Harvard Business School Press -2000

important example of the corporation's choice to liberate or ignore. Foremen, operatives, sales people, marketers, accountants and bookkeepers may all have their visions of improvement. The issue is how to release these talents into practice?

The job description dimension ensures that the mechanics of the business are managed. The vision issues at all levels help move us beyond the mechanics to concepts. Encouraging conceptualising at all levels in the business creates a few problems, but more importantly, many opportunities for continuous improvement to existing and emerging processes. Additionally a positive and intensely integrated corporate whole is in the making. Each part, where it chooses, thinks and becomes part of the functioning brain of the body corporate. Vision and initiative are no longer the sole remit of the leadership; these are shared throughout the 'thinking organisation'. At every level management is encouraged to think about purpose and end games in addition to the means of doing things.

The problems come in handling all these new initiatives and concepts. If the thinking organisation is to flourish then transparent adjudication and open-minded reception of new ideas is a must. This is an onerous and demanding protocol. It needs organisation; it needs continuous enthusiasm and flexible application. Most important of all it needs to empower the peer groups or inner ring relations who are frequently the best judges of the effectiveness of the new ideas. If you want to dig coal ask a face worker for his advice.

Hand on Heart:

- Do we feel that there is a true freedom of expression in our workplace?
- Do our people have the health of the Body Corporate as a real conscious concern?
- Do the bosses listen?

Section 4

The Culture Map and Corporate Muscle

If the corporation is to succeed, it must be made up of individuals who in turn seek to make a difference to overall performance. People who contribute though, are more difficult to work with, than those who are happy enough 'to drift along' and do only what is expected from them. I assume those that read this book belong to the former category.

There are two issues here; one for the Human Resource planning and recruiting policy, and one for the aspiring executive. We talked of style and culture[4] of the organisation earlier; here we come to the nub.

Recruiting and developing talented individuals is the ground on which the company stands or falls. However it is seldom that we see ourselves in a static situation where we can read the future with any certainty. Indeed the speed of change is increasing and our choices become more and more complicated. However it is worth plotting what we might call a culture map. This table (fig 3) is a guide and focuses on a simple example of a food company that sees the need to change. The map incorporates a review of HR as well as actions and time fences; thus creating an action plan of aspirations or corporate goals that measures and feels the people profile and strengths required to succeed.

This might not be the traditional view of 'culture' but it does give us a lead and an idea of the corporate profile and the HR needs for survival and growth. It also gives us a chance to take stock of our HR, our need to strengthen or change. It does not substitute for HR audit and individual and group appraisal.

Reverting to the contributing individual, he or she has to believe that they can make a difference. It is not a matter of if, but how? Our individual contributors in their liberated individually centred organisations want to feel and see that they make a difference. They want to get a buzz from their daily work existence. True, perhaps not every day, but even the struggles and the drudgery must be for a purpose. They must have some ownership of that purpose.

Further there should be a clear recognition of individual strengths; this after all is the neutron of their atomic existence. The combination and freeing of individual talent and strengths will give the corporation its strength and muscle, not only for intellectual weight but also for speed and responsiveness. Effective performance is not only the delivery of a difference, but a difference in the fastest possible time. An organisation cannot be effective without speed to market, and then speed to market again.

---

[4] Edgar Schien – OrganisationalCulure & Leadership - Paperback

Fig.**3**. Culture Map: With actions and time fences.

Core roots: e.g. Technology, service etc..	Key Markets:	Market leadership: Strongest segment	Aspirations: (where to next?)
i.e. I.T., Chemistry, e.g retail food,(what ever)	Main existing market e.g. Food Manufacturing..	As above; e.g. Pre-packed vegetables to supermarkets.	Rational view of future shape of the business i.e. Widen range into frozen fruit & vegetables.
How strong are we in our skills base? Where does it need strengthening? E.g. We need more expertise in freezing technology.	Time horizon to sustain this market, (be aggressive it's shorter than you think). Need to launch new range within 18 months.	How are we to strengthen our hold?(if you can't be prepared to move fast). Revise brand marketing.	How fast do we need to move? Review Advertising marketing internal and external resources.
What are the new skills we need now and in the short term? Review existing technical and marketing strengths. NOW	Have we the right people to defend and sustain? We need to strengthen marketing as well as recruit technologists for the frozen food initiative.3 Months.	Have we the people to improve and increase market share? Review training requirements and implement for new recruits, > 3 months	Do we have the flexibility for new venturing? Nominate and empower responsible senior exec to steer the change,

Hand on Heart:

- Do we have a culture map that takes us from our roots to aspirations?
- Is the talent we have consistent with attaining our goals?
- Are we as fast on our feet as we should be?
- Are our people entrusted to use their initiative?

Section 5

One thing at a time.

The word 'Focus', it is so often misused. It is true that we can do one thing at a time better than trying to do many things at once. It is seldom possible to do several jobs well at the same time and on time. Despite this common wisdom, most executives spend a good deal of their allotted work time trying to juggle umpteen jobs at once. Not surprisingly under these conditions we settle for 'second best', or 'adequate' or 'best we can do for now'.

The more senior the executive, with the fewer but broader responsibilities, expect their reports to deliver a bewildering number of completed tasks within artificial time constraints that have little or nothing to do with the jobholder's workload. The strangulating effect of calendared meetings and reports take no account of individual workloads. Time is gobbled up in an endless round of pointless rituals, forcing individuals to squeeze more tasks into less time. Instead of appointing individuals to solve problems through their own informal team structures, the organisation is suffocated through traditional hierarchical reporting.

The cry 'Focus' is often used as an excuse for the passing down of an unshared 'vision' that seldom has the backing of the whole body corporate. "Focus on this – don't think!" It shuts out the thinking individual, neuters the non-conformist and deadening enthusiasm. It removes ownership from those individual centres that are the strength of the business.

Individual priority choice is desirable but not always practical. Executives have to make choices and rank those tasks and issues that need attention to achieve key results. They must decide what is most important and what will be the measurable results of this task or that. The higher in the decision making chain, the fewer but broader the issues, more intense the work and the judgements. But no matter where the individual is centred it is always better to concentrate on one job at a time.

Concentration on individual tasks will achieve more than chaotic attempts to solve a range of problems at the same time. There is a temptation to spend too much time solving yesterday's problems than thinking of tomorrow's opportunities. For example most companies agonise over the abandonment of dying product lines. They should of be spending that time instead on substitutes and innovation. Even though it's easy to see the end of a product line it's amazing that so much energy goes into sustaining the unsustainable.

It is inordinately difficult to put away yesterday, and think of tomorrow. Of course there are lessons from our past, but they should be learned and then we must move on. It's in the moving on that our priorities must lie. Alas in the pressure cooker of reporting last month's figures and a plethora of other historical data, we dither in a maelstrom of non decisive behaviour that advances the corporate goals not one jot.

This is where we need to learn to concentrate, the past is a useful data bank of experience for operational improvement but it is an insecure springboard to the future. Walking away from problems is easy, but walking away from success is much harder. History is history we can learn from success and failure, but the elimination of the latter and the repetition of the former will not guarantee our future.

We have to break the stranglehold of routine and apply our apt priorities. This means allowing individuals to solve their prescribed and agreed priorities in realistic time spans that are not otherwise cluttered with useless routine and backward analysis. Then and only then can we expect first class solutions or work. Only the best should do if the jobholder is allowed to give his or her undivided attention to the challenge of today's problems and tomorrow's promise.

Hands on Heart:

- Do we expect too much from our people?
- Has everyone got adequate time to concentrate on priorities?
- Can we cut out unnecessary routine to ease their burden?
- Do we respect other people's work loads?

Section 6

Decisions, decisions.

The body Corporate is a living organism. Its purpose is to live and grow, just like any other. Living means solvency, and growth means exactly what it says. To remain solvent let alone grow the corporation has to achieve earnings through selling, adding value, investing etc. To do any of these things it must effect actions. It must make things happen, the right things. If nothing is made to happen inevitably the corporation will perish, starved of income; it will die sooner than later.

Such decisions[5] should be made for only a small number of reasons. That is; that actions will be taken to improve, sustain or defend income. Exceptionally one can decide to leave an issue, but even then there should be a decision on time fences. A decision is worthless without resultant action.

There are decisions to be made at every level of the business[6]. The Board might decide it is necessary to cut expenditure. The Director of finance might decide to look for savings in administration. The Departmental head might decide to save on consumables. The Purchasing Manager may decide to buy fewer pencils. The decisions become more precise as we descend the degree of executive responsibility. The choices left to each level become narrower and narrower; thus easier to make. The key issues here, are that the resultant actions, probably numerous actions, save expenditure in many departments, fulfilling the purpose of the decision.

The first issue was it necessary to make a decision at all? What's right? What's wrong? What's the difference? Are we really clear about the basic premise, do we have a handle on the solution parameters? After all there's a great difference between let's save expenditure of a million dollars or pounds rather than let's save as much as we can. The million dollars is a definition of the problem parameter, 'as much as we can' on the other hand can lead to inconsistent actions down the executive line.

Whatever decision we face, it must be based on a hypothesis of the likely outcome of action. Before we act we should as far as possible test the hypothesis. I do not mean by this that we should endlessly examine the minutiae of the facts contributing to the analysis, but we do need peer group testing, so that all the actions resulting from decisions, at whatever level, result in rational consequences and within the parameters of our hypothesis.

All this sounds dry and academic, because the decision making body; 'the brains of the body corporate' are made up of very disparate human beings. The consequence is that the decisions are frequently not entirely based on facts and analysis, but on intuition, emotion, as well as the rational and the well informed. Interestingly, the fact is that the well-informed and rational decisions are sometimes less effective that the intuitive and the emotional. Intuition and emotional inputs tend often to be

---

[5]

[6] Peter Drucker's - The elements of decision making; The effective Executive

creative and more lateral than the rationally well informed. Most corporations fail to capitalise on these creative forces, are wary of them and suppress that type of thinking. There is a need to recognise these qualities as virtues and we need to learn to suspend our judgement long enough to entertain these unorthodox views. Once we hear them without prejudice, then we can test them against the hypothesis.

Courage, imagination and creativity are all part of the armoury of decision-making, unless of course if we fail to act.

Therefore when a decision has been reached, act, if the decision is invalid abandon it, but do not fudge.

Hand on Heart:

- Do we act on all our decisions?

- Do we concentrate on decisions that result in actions on Key Result Areas?

- Do we second guess other people's decisions and waste time?

- Do we spend time on making decisions that do not matter?

Section 7

Summary : Individual and corporate effectiveness

- Know your job and what's expected from you, change what needs changing, agree this with your boss, understand the inner ring relationships.

- Respect the organisation and your responsibility to fit and network effectively, remember you are at the centre of your organisation.

- Measure how you use your time; review your time diary at least twice a year.

- Do not call meetings if an individual can be briefed to solve a problem.

- Use your strengths; get a buzz from your input.

- Be a thinking contributor.

- Where possible do one thing at a time. Respect other people's workload

- Concentrate on key issues.

- Make decisions that need to be made.

- If you don't act you've not effected a decision.

- Test your decisions against the result parameters in the hypothesis..

- Find out why there are other views.

- Courage, you're rewarded for effectiveness. Not always just that which you find enjoyable.

- You cannot remain successful by not changing, and not making decisions that lead to change.

- He who does not make decisions does not make mistakes, except that he is killing the business.

- Act, do it!

Chapter 2

Change; the constant variable.

Section 1

Change, The first Constant.

Change: Let's discuss the nature of change as it applies to us as individuals as well as to our businesses.

Change is a small word but is one of the most potent in the dictionary. Change implies something new, something that did not apply before, maybe not new in the absolute sense but new to our organisation or us.

Change also implies a time dimension[7], this is what we did before, and this is what we do now. There is a definite point in time when the change in behaviour or thinking took hold. There are two periods; before and after; the paradigm shift

Change is punctuation in time. Of course we are used to telling the time by the clock and the calendar. However there are many clocks ticking which dictate a relative time; Personal bio-clocks, environmental clocks, political clocks, OPEC clocks, technology clocks, financial clocks. These clocks may be ticking more loudly inside your organisation or outside the organisation.

The problem with all these clocks is that we cannot see or hear all of them.

One thing we can be sure about all the clocks is that they will not stop and they will not go into reverse.

Despite our lack of awareness, all these clocks signify an inevitable change in our environment, even if we can't see them or touch them.

Time is a constant (K1), which inexorably ticks on, something that none of us can avoid, we cannot save it, nor can we bank or borrow it. Time, in a way rules us, and everything we know. Nothing escapes Time except Time itself.

Hands on Heart:

- Do we know which clocks are important to us?
- Do we keep a constant eye on K1?

---

[7] Culture Shift - Price Pritchett – Pritchett & Associates Inc.

Section 2

The constant need.

As time passes we need to sustain ourselves. That, as they say, is life. Corporate life is no different, just as you and I need food, air and water to sustain us. So our organisations need to be sustained by Income. Income is the food of corporate survival **(K2).**

Here is the central premise of business, the sustenance of adequate income over time. This is not to imply that the purpose of business is to make money, it is not. The purpose of making money is to sustain and nurture the business. If I were writing this paper in Germany or Japan, this would be taken as read. However in the UK and USA businesses are still treated as assets to be bought and sold, despite the fact that the assets of modern day business are increasingly intellectual property. Shareholders need to learn that these assets need respect and can no longer be taken for granted as fixed, these assets can vote with their feet.

It's all very well reading the theory, the almost non-stop flow of management blurb that cascades onto our desks, but unless we constantly focus on the maintenance of the (K2) lifeblood of the corporation we are lost.

We can express K2 in a number of directly related ways i.e. Surplus income after Cost of Sales plus expenses, or Return on Capital employed. Either example will do perfectly well, the key issue is that we take a measure that cannot be fudged, and we use it consistently to measure our corporate performance.

Hands on Heart:

- Do we fudge the K1/K2 judgement?
- Are we realistic about periodic phasing of budgets?
- Do we *do* something when K1/K2 slips?

Section 3

A Continuous process

In the context of change management, although we acknowledge the constant movement and changing of time we just can't abandon yesterday, and cast off into the unknown. Change management is not a stop start process; rather it is a process of constant evolution to meet the inevitably changing circumstances. This means we must have the ability **to** change what is already being done just as much as the ability to do new and different things. The future has to be created from the present.

We have to acknowledge that we cannot be master of all that changes. Things happen to our businesses, on the one hand and we make things happen on the other.

Situations therefore can be divided into events that demand a reactive and proactive response.

Life is about pitching and catching, pitching is by and large more comfortable than catching. Despite this most of us, are less prepared to risk a pitch, which is within our control, to making a catch, which relies on external initiative. The skills required to initiate and to react intelligently are quite different, and the embodiment of these skills under one corporate roof is unusual. Learning to manage change and to be comfortable with it certainly makes these skills necessary.

The changes that come from external sources can be both positive and negative.

If we were asked to list those external change catalysts, which we easily recall, we are more likely to sight negative than positive experiences. This is because we associate good things as a consequence of our own actions and bad things as the consequences of someone else's. In short the natural human condition is to deny responsibility for mistakes and accept responsibilities for success.

One of the first demands of effective change management is to recognise and to square up to those events that are plainly within our compass to influence. These are often perceived as external influences but they are in truth internal, we should not be in catching mode but in pitching mode. Examples of these are easy to recall:

- The Sales forecasts, heavily year end loaded, that are never quite delivered; or the output promises that never quite make it; (rationalised as the consequence of external factors.)
- The cash flow that doesn't materialise;
- The debts that we don't collect.

Here is a clear responsibility to change the things we do now, this is the today on which tomorrow will be built. The imperative to change those areas that deter from achieving income per unit of time never goes away; the wastes of resources that are involved in rescuing the organisation or repairing institutional mistakes exhaust and weaken the body corporate. We must never allow custom and practice to dilute the ratio of **K2/K1**. These organisational weaknesses commit valuable resources to non-results.

It is imperative that individuals continuously face up to meeting their commitments to the corporation. The function of executives and managers is to facilitate maximum corporate performance; failure to deliver promises is absolutely contrary to this goal. We have to live in an environment where everyone strives to deliver on promises; a promise made is a debt unpaid.

Hand on Heart:

- How often do we get caught on the hop? Too often, never?
- Do we face up to deficiencies of our own making?
- Are we quick enough to respond to external forces?

Section 4

Continuous improvement.

Recognising those elements of the business that do not contribute is a skill not widely shared. The theorists are unequivocal about dumping old products and equipment. I would be more sanguine. It is a rare quality of judgement and courage, which discontinues products or dumps written off assets at the right time. The prospect of abandoning traditional core business is frightening, especially so if you have no idea how you are to replace these old favourites. If, however, you remember that the only constants in the changing world, is **K1** time and **K2** the need for income stream then at least you have the beginnings of a reliable theorem which will help in making those very difficult decisions.

According to Drucker[8] we would ask the question of every product and service, "If we did not do this already, would we, knowing what we know now, go into it?" If the answer is no, he says, "What do we do now?" He answers, "Abandon it." Again I believe that that can be the right answer but that practical reality seldom makes such abandonment easy.

To start the process the alternative view is to set a Time fence by which the organisation compensates for the discontinuation, with the minimum goal of income per unit of time being equal to the outgoing product or service, but with potential that satisfies the investment criteria. **See figure 4:**

---

[8] Peter Drucker – The effective Executive- Harper Business

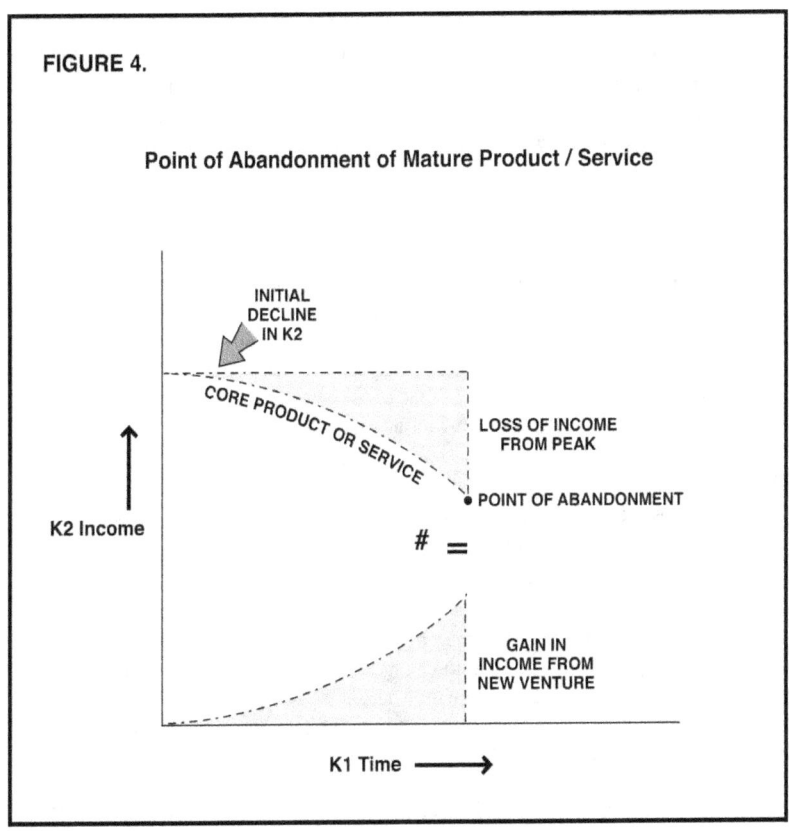

FIGURE 4.

Point of Abandonment of Mature Product / Service

INITIAL DECLINE IN K2

CORE PRODUCT OR SERVICE

LOSS OF INCOME FROM PEAK

POINT OF ABANDONMENT

K2 Income

=

GAIN IN INCOME FROM NEW VENTURE

K1 Time

The issue here is to recognise the real causes of declining income K2, we have to face up to the negative forces that inevitably devalue mature products or services. We see the need to defend but we do not see the cost of defence as a real cost, we just see the falling margins and spend huge resources shoring up the volume results. These are real negative defensive costs. They do not appear in the accounts but they are more important and intrusive than any other cost largely because they are not planned and there is no limit to our pursuit of sustaining the falling star.

If in the event we recognise the early signs of product or service maturity and face our own responsibility to replace the mature line, then such a practice would foresee the end of product and capital life cycles, thus enshrining change reviews well before the slow death of many of our so called core products or services. This is the kind of problem that motor car manufacturers struggle with all the time, the stakes are huge and many have suffered terminally because they've failed to instigate model change at the right time. Once the process has become institutionalised it is easy to maintain. Where perhaps the theorists fail in their advice, is in their assumption that initial choices are made in sterile circumstances, rather than in the heat of battle.

Reacting to externally imposed change:

Lets face it, most of the time where ever or who ever we are, Change is imposed on you by external events. We are reacting. Usually we react and instigate change as a result of negative events. We have lost an order, the stock is too high, our web page has a drastically lower hit rate, and quality is down, etc., etc.

The normal or usual response to setbacks is to ignore them, only when problems become unavoidably pressing do we react. Often knee jerk or panic is the response.

This situation is the one that none of the intellectual giants refer to. Why should they? Surely this is a simple problem to solve. It is. But unless we adopt a systematic approach to addressing these sorts of issues then they will continue to take us by surprise. The other characteristic of our response to these nasty surprises, which of course shouldn't be surprises at all, is that instinctively negative response. Cut back, fire people, slash stocks, and burn new initiatives.

Instead our response can be more positive:
• What can we learn from the experience?
• What reinforcements would make a difference?
• What staff training and development would eliminate this problem?

We know that no matter how perfect we are as senior or middle managers that these events are going to arise. We have to change our behaviour so that those with whom we work can face these issues, not with a fear and dread, but safe in the knowledge that we will as a team learn from our mistakes. This learning culture doesn't excuse or encourage lassitude rather it encourages effort.

As well as keeping an eye on K1/K2, the systematic control and analysis of our response and improvement, to external changes is a must. This naturally leads us into the fields of continuous improvement and quality assurance, which hopefully we all embrace.

The business and philosophy of continuous improvement[9], requires a commitment from the top to the bottom of the organisation[10], to a ceaseless labour that so very few corporations sustain. In some ways it's easier to see the need to improve when things are not going too well rather than when things are going very well. That is why companies fall off the perch of success so often. The intoxication of success diminishes the desire to continually improve.

The question remains; How do we systematically and continually improve? This is not the forum to go into detail, for there are many agencies devoted to just this subject. Suffice it to say that if your enterprise is not practicing some degree of constant and continuous improvement programmes then it is not long for this world. This ideal is the fundamental basis for effective change management.

---

[9] Kaizen- see Japanese method of incremental improvement
[10] Michael Brassard – The Memory Jogger 11 – Goal/QPC

The K1/K2 relation never leaves us. However, there is a danger in the concept of learning only from our mistakes, for that can turn into a hyper-analytical organisation that looks only backwards.

We must also learn to change, not only by correcting faults and putting right mistakes, but by seeking new and better ways of doing things. This latter initiative demands that we build in a positive way; emphasising and reinforcing our success and strengths. In some ways this is easier to manage, although the encouragement of success has to be kept in balance. Repair and maintenance of the business must be progressive not routine, for it is the routine that leads to atrophy.

The Rules for Continuous improvement:

1 Attend to mistakes – How can we systemise these mistakes out.?

Continuous improvement requires a high degree of analytical skill, a clear view of our past actions, an aptitude for detail, the finisher's dedication, and the gift of application. Here we need dogged enthusiasm, a comfort searching the detail. This is where that part of the team who are the valuable and reliable administrators take centre stage.

2 Log our successes, - How can we build on them?

Change also has to embrace the dimension on the other side of now, the future. In some ways the attributes to continuously improve on the one hand and to innovate on the other are contradictory. Building on success, improving a winning formula has one foot firmly on the past but the other stretching to the future.

Hands on Heart:

- Are we learning from our successes and our mistakes?
- Do we review periodically our performance and decide improvement actions?
- What changes have we made that we all recognise?

Section 5

Looking Forward

Innovation is the current 'buzz word' and much misunderstood. Innovation can mean 'Eureka' the discovery of a revolutionary new product and service, but this is rare. Just as continuous improvement can lead to genuine innovation, so innovation itself can be systematically induced. The idea that innovation is entirely inspirational is wide of the mark. Systematic approaches to innovation can and do result in changes which move businesses and careers forward.

Newness is very attractive on the one hand but can be very threatening on the other. If an innovation is born as a consequence of crisis it is often a bad one. This is because the drive to do something 'new' is driven by something akin to panic, i.e. we must try something different, without defining the result parameters. Novelty alone should not be seen as a constructive innovative step.

Keep in mind that our eventual goal is to sustain and improve the K1/K2 ratios. The most common panic response to an uncertain future is the slash and burn, to save on resources expenditure and employee liability. The idea of managing the same business with fewer resources is seen as a way to improve performance. This is seldom a way towards long term improvement. Again beyond the saving of resources there are seldom plans to sustain the levels of income or indeed to invest those savings in future development. If, as often is the case, the K1/K2 relationship is not kept in focus, and the cut backs are a response in panic, they often signal the decline and the demise of the enterprise.

We're talking about change[11], and some Managers seem to grab the idea that change is good, therefore let's change something, anything, for the sake of change. Even at the top of the largest corporations, CEO's suffer the same temptations. They ask themselves, "are we doing well enough, and are we changing fast enough?" They frequently get consultants to report back, and the consultants of course, feel obliged to recommend a change programme which is frequently suited to, more work for the consultant, rather than the needs of the corporation.

Before we instigate change we must ask ourselves; "What will the benefits be to us and our customers?" "As a consequence, what about K1/K2 and what are the time fences we must meet?"

The other common response to adverse change is to reorganise. You and your department and companies do need to reorganise from time to time, however we need to do it for a positive purpose, which can clearly understand. Quitting a dying product line is preferable to a sequence of reorganisations, trying to keep the dead alive.

Action is often confused with positive change, when it is the very opposite. Busy fools do not improve the K1/K2 ratios.

---

[11] Bernard Burns – Managing Change – Prentice Hall

These response types to negative external change, such as loss of business, poorer margins, productivity drops, all call for good leadership, and good analysis of the real cause of the set backs. Often these setbacks can be made up through the systematic application of our continuous improvement programmes. Sometimes, however, we have to recognise that the business, product or process really is at the end of the line, so we've got to let it go. Let it go and move onto something new that can get us back to improving that K1/K2.

Hand on Heart:

- When faced with falling K1/K2 do we think of cutting back?
- Do we look to positive responses to profit falls?
- Do we face up to reducing or aborting redundant products?
- Do we have plans to replace redundant products and services?

Section 6

Leaders and followers.

All of us have at least one influence that will cause us negative change; Competitors! These guys get up every morning and set out to get the better of us, we'd better believe it. This is one of the most important influences of change. A change leader[12] is usually the market leader and has the reputation of being the first with new products and ideas. This is what we'd all like our companies to be. The change leader has a very low experience of negative externally imposed changes, but a high experience of exciting positive changes that he has instigated. Here is a company that grasps and sustains the initiative.

How do they do it? The 64000$ question!

Here's what they do: Hand on Heart
- They practice continuous improvement, on internal operations.
- They know their competitors' every move, and are quick to respond.
- They watch the clocks.
- They make sure they get the best bang for their buck.
- They innovate systematically; they introduce changes that are not necessarily big, but always effective. The innovations are manageable and deliverable. They never change or venture more than one dimension at a time, i.e. market, service, technology, or media/material.
- They communicate well; every one in the company is involved and is comfortable with a changing environment. Communicating is a way of life.
- They have the people who can deliver.

The body Corporate: The successes and the failures:

Change leaders we've seen are those who can perform the above consistently well. Why is it then, that so many companies fail? Why are there so few companies that are change leaders? Many of them have splendid CEO's the nicest, hardest working, people you're likely to meet. Many have good traditional organisations, many have seen good times, but few sustain their leadership for any length of time.

The most common reason that companies decline is that they only get one idea during their existence; usually this idea was the reason why the company was formed. That idea may hold good for a number of months or years, and variations will have been introduced from time to time. However, eventually that original idea is swamped by competitors or simply overtaken by other technologies or substitutes. Even companies based on advanced technologies are just as prone to this kind of decline.

---

[12] Bill George – Authentic Leadership – Jossy Bass Wiley

What makes the difference between ephemeral and long term success?   If we accept that the criteria we've discussed is at least part of the success, then why don't others survive and thrive more frequently? What makes the difference?

Hand on Heart:

- Do you practice all of the ideas in the list: -?

Section 7

The Human Resource..

What is different about every company is their people. Not only the sum of their talent but the way the organisation recognises and allows the talent that exists to flourish. If we think of the body corporate in a human analogy, then we would see that a successful human being is a good thinker, a good worker, an enthusiast, and a driver, a mover and a shaker.

He thinks with his disciplined but flexible brain; he works hard with a fit body; he's an enthusiast with 'heart'; and he's a mover and shaker because he shows leadership.

How many companies integrate these qualities in their teams? They need to think through good strategies and clearly communicate them through slim yet effective organisations, with demonstrable decisive and respected leadership. In the thinking and doing part of the organisation, they have the grafters and the inventors, that can manage the routine and the unexpected.

These qualities have to work in a number of dimensions[13]:
- Learning and reacting to experience. Ideas from data.
- Responding to external happenings. Reactions to events.
- Creating new ideas. Hypothesis from ideas.

These are the conditions:
- Responding to what we know. Reacting to data.
- Responding to that which we could reasonably expect. Testing hypothesis.
- Going beyond that which we know, even into regions of which we have no experience at all. Having ideas and taking risk.

Hand on Heart:

- How does your team stack up on brain, heart and muscle?
- Do you review – 'What next' options?

---

[13] de Bono – Lateral Thinking for Managers – Mc Graw-Hill

Section 8

No escape from Risk.

Risk[14] is defined as; taking a chance; acting where the result of your action in not predictable, acting in spite of the possibility of loss or injury. Risk is uncomfortable, and by definition should be avoided. Risking the worth of the corporation is contrary to the duties of Directors, and risk that ends up with an adverse result is likely to be judged as irresponsible.

Risks that result in an advantage to the corporation on the other hand are applauded as entrepreneurial skill, gifted judgement, brilliant deduction and fine business sense.

However the consequences of risk pan out; there is always a rational hindsight that evaluates the risk in terms of a qualified action. If the results are good; then the risk taker will claim insight or inside knowledge. If the results are bad; the risk taker will claim adverse external factors, usually a confluence of unpredictable misfortune.

He takes too many risks, she is too risk averse, this is a risky adventure, this has little or no risk attached to it. These are common comments on both people and actions. Risk analysis has passed into a whole discipline of its own; we can expect degrees to be conferred in the discipline. A doctorate in Risk Analysis is not as surreal as it seems; it will study the possibility of taking risk out of risk.

Yet everything we do has some degree of risk attached to it. Even doing nothing in the face of change, is to almost guarantee the demise of the corporation. If survival and growth are our goals can we possibly achieve them without a high degree of risk?

Here is another great irony, if your corporation is lead by those who are unwilling to take any risk; there is only the exercise of negative power, sadly without the leadership qualities of honest decisiveness to make that power positive. Here are the leaders who are not leaders at all. They cower behind the power vested in them, they are afraid of change and find it impossible to trust anyone's judgement but their own. That of course is easy; since they seldom decide anything of worth. The response to these sorts of corporations is the creation of vast bureaucracies where permission to take any initiative, is almost impossible to get. The majority of the people in the organisation are bound by checks and balances at every turn. The saddest thing is that the checkers and the balancers have no responsibility other than to eliminate risk. The creative will is systematically stamped and an army of yes men and women follow the risk-averse leadership into the black hole of nowhere.

This kind of organisation is concerned with negative power. You can't do this or that because this or that may happen. You must submit a plan that weighs at least five pounds, and a panel of 'professionals will assess its worth'. Ideas are like explosives they have to be isolated, made safe and then disposed of.

---

[14] R Max Wideman - Project & Program Management – Project Management Institute

Do you recognise these symptoms? Are you in a position to change attitudes such as these? If you recognise them and you can do nothing about them, change your employer. If you recognise them and can do something about them, do it now.

Here we have a company that is growing at a phenomenal rate, things are going extremely well, here we take risks, here we have no checks and balances; everyone is allowed to do as they like. This kind of organisation teeters on the brink of anarchy, power has been liberated, yes, but for what common purpose and for what corporate goal? The international traders in the international banking community live every close to these conditions where risk taking is the nub of their very corporate raison d'etre. Here the checks and balances are meant to put limits on the degree of risk that any trader may undertake, failure to spot over trading is disastrous. (Barings, to a lesser extent Bank of Ireland.)

Interestingly the dealers who overtrade seldom do it for personal gain. Usually it is one trade more; to recoup former mistakes, like a gambler chasing his losses. The organisations encourage this since every dealer is driven by incentive based on trade gains. Failure to meet goals results in job loss, so the dealer is jammed into a high pressure corner, to exercise risk to gain but only so much. The rewards are high but the stresses on the dealers are immense.

This illustrates commercial life in general, although the risk pressures are generally under less time pressure. There has to be an appropriate amount of risks whatever the corporation's business.

Risk is unavoidable if an organisation is to act positively and move its fortune forward. There is always a degree of risk that is appropriate to the business, and the liabilities and assets that are at stake. Some would say that the larger the organisation the greater the tendency to the negative exercise of power and loss of leadership; in smaller organisations the higher the risk taking. This may be appropriate. The following figure illustrates that the executive has choices in the expression of negative or positive power. Whilst it would be nice to able to assert that the practice of positive power is always appropriate, clearly there are times when Management's judgement has to prevail even to limit risk or to contain error. However the figure illustrates the culture and attitude differences that prevail in both extremes. There is no question that a culture of positive power leadership is more fun to work in than the opposite, but fun is not everything.

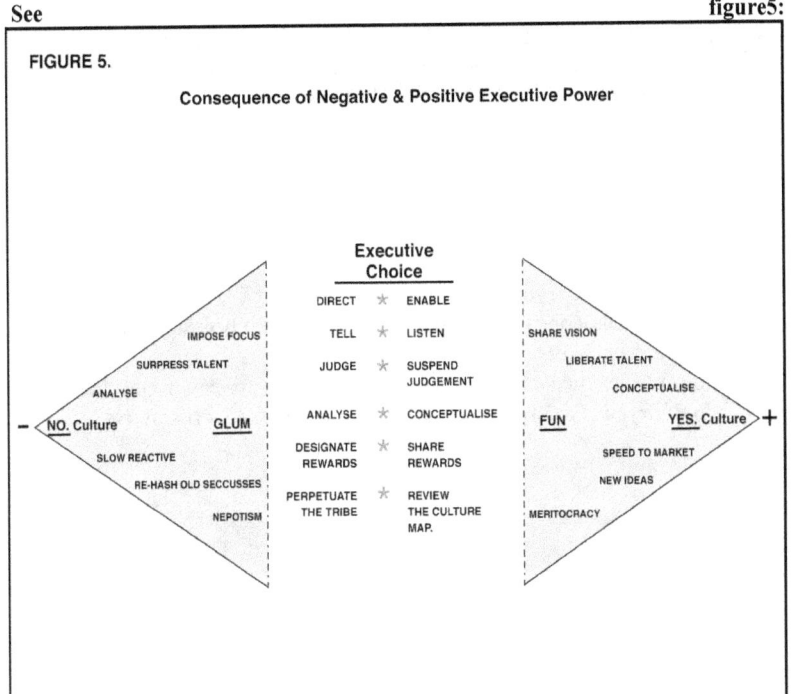

FIGURE 5.

Consequence of Negative & Positive Executive Power

Is this inevitable? Can the larger corporation avoid the negative risk aversion that in its turn risks paralysis and atrophy?

A CEO of a large corporation may well think himself to be a open minded balanced risk taker who leads by example, yet those further down the line may believe their employers to be risk averse and heavily reliant on negative power. There are two principle reasons for this dichotomy; 1 the type and shape of the organisation, and 2 the type of people who inhabit it.

Strict hierarchies do not communicate well in an upward direction. By their very nature the tablets are passed down from the mountain as if by divine right. The messages may start with the best intentions and most liberal and noble sentiments, but unless there is a meaningful dialogue the message will be conditioned as it comes down through each level of command. Inevitably the message will be spun and spun again so that the sentiment if not the content is much changed. If the transmitter of the message has no influence or part in the message then there can be no meaningful dialogue at each level. The result is a game of Chinese whispers.

However in a ring matrix environment each inner ring community will discuss and seek involvement in ideas no matter what their source. The reactions and subsequent discussions are easily and naturally fed back to the source. Risk is assessed at multiple levels and valuable insights are gained from across the organisation.

It's important that the less formal structure works at a number of levels simultaneously so that the defenders against new ideas or perceived risk are not allowed to block progress with the exercise of negative power.

Hand on Heart:

- Is it fun to work in your company?
- Would you describe your corporation as predominantly positive or negative?
- Do you really have two way communications?
- How often are juniors asked about problem solving, or improvement ideas?
- How are you in a risk environment, balanced, relaxed, or risk averse?

Section 9

The Team most likely to succeed.

We have seen the necessity of facing a number of different types of changes, from the external 'clocks', the deadly competitor, continuous improvement, and creative development. The corporate response requires an array of skills, and different aptitudes. If we are to succeed then we have to develop these complimentary skills departmentally and company wide.

Leadership needs to recognise these differences[15] and create effective teams that possess these complementary skills. As individuals we should recognise our own strengths and the strengths in others. This is probably the most difficult area of all to manage. Each of us has a view of his or her ability and talents; it is seldom we recognise the strengths and talents of others.

Being creative is often considered a desirable attribute, but the practice of creative change is rarely welcome. New ideas are dangerous, new ideas are all right if they are ours, but seldom acceptable if they come from a third party. Above all new ideas pose risk. Why should I take risk for his idea?

"What a silly idea!"

"We tried it before, it didn't work!"

"That's not new we thought of it years ago!"

Rejection is the natural response of most people. I wonder if new ideas are so readily rejected in Microsoft or 3M's, or does their culture naturally require reflection and consideration of new ideas?

Management's job[16] is to create a working environment that liberates all the talents, those that create, those that slog away at the detail of continual improvement, those that react aggressively to competitive pressure, and that analyse opportunity and risk. These all have value, they are all vital to manage change effectively and to ensure that K1/K2 remain in step.

Such teams in smaller operations need to be flexible and multidisciplined, larger corporations need to ensure that there is a balance of resources for the established, the evolving and the future. Every company should put aside in its budget a sum for investment into future developments not only such as R&D, but also for the specific purpose of creating new opportunity.

It's no good enjoying the good times without investing in the future and it's no good scrapping innovation in the bad times because that's your only hope of any future at

---

[15] Thomas F Crum – The Magic of Conflict – Simon & Schuster
[16] Thomas R Keen – Creating effective and Successful teams – Perdue university Press

all. Yet this is the single most common reason for company failures, failing to manage change.

Even in the soundest company, where all these principles are put into practice, there will remain the problem that such continuous change which will be exciting for some, but disconcerting for others.

It is imperative therefore that change leaders be excellent communicators and great motivators if they are to continue winning in the uncertain but exciting opportunity that is tomorrow.

Hand on Heart:

- Is there respect for the different talents in your business, or do we favour one discipline above others?
- Is our team balanced with a range of quality talent?
- Are your company responses to change well managed, is the team motivated?

Section 10

Summary

To summarise this chapter, I cannot do better than quote from Charles Handy's 'Beyond Certainty' he said this:

"In a time of change we must always question whether the things that used to work, will work so well in future. We must not be slaves to our histories but trustees to our destinies. Our businesses are too precious to be lost because we have not dared to question the past, or to dream the future. Let us start before it is too late."

Chapter 3

Culture, the prison of experience.

Section 1

Definitions.

It is said that Culture defines what is expected from us; both individually and as a group. It is the paradigm in which we live. It pervades every thing we do and conditions our expectations. What is it then that is so powerful? Is the straight jacket of cultural definition for ever set?

If we accept that we live in times of exponential change, when we see for example, the world population growing more in the next fifty years than it has the last seven million and information technology advancing more in the last year than in the whole of our history, if not in empiric discovery, then certainly in technical development. In this context, what is the relevance of this thing we call culture?

The dictionary defines culture as the manifestation of human intellectual achievement regarded collectively. The customs, arts, social institutions and achievements of a particular social group. The definition is firmly built on past experience.

No one would deny the virtues of some cultures, nor the reality of cultural influence. To be 'cultured' is after all generally a compliment. Yet here is a great paradox; for we have to conform to be accepted into our chosen group at work, or socially, by accepting the rules; 'the social institutions'. Yet in these times of enormous change, is this rational?

Perhaps we would do well to alter our definition of culture to; the manifestations of human intellectual *aspirations* regarded collectively. The customs, arts, social institutions, achievements *and aspirations* of a particular social group. These changes do much to shift the basis of our definition from the past to the future, more dynamism and less reverential to the past.

Even if we succeed in changing the definition to more of a forward-looking premise, we still have a deeply rooted institutional belief in the value of ancient culture. Ancient in modern industrial terms can be ten years, or in national cultures a thousand. I am not suggesting that we pay no respect to history and the achievements of those who have gone before; I am just facing the dilemma of living in times of such enormous and sweeping change.

The term 'culture shock' seeks to define reaction to culture change. The feeling of disorientation experienced when we are suddenly subjected to unfamiliar culture, or set of attitudes. Or when we feel he need to question existing mind-sets and perceived values. Here's the nub, how do we take the shock out of culture change[17]?

Hand on Heart:

- What is the culture of your organisation?. Can you describe or categorise it?
- What needs to change?

---

[17]Cameron & Quinn - Diagnosing & changing organizational culture

Section 2

How well are we equipped?

In our own corporations can we say that we are fit to handle the changes that are bound to beset us? Yes, bound to beset us. Does our record indicate that we're changing close to the required rate? Does our prevailing culture even allow us to answer these questions honestly? On what basis can we make the judgement?

Here are some questions we must ask ourselves, and answer honestly.

- Is our return on average capital employed (adjusted for inflation) increasing?
- In steady to growth markets are we gaining market share?
- What are doing to replace no-growth market involvement?
- Are our brightest people happy?

At least here the shareholder has a real role to play, bye and large the markets read company performances without romance or sentiment. That is as it should be.

Beyond the shareholder view there ought to be a more honest self-appraisal, a ruthless comparison with competition, with no excuses. We have to face up to our own discomfiture.

When things are not going well; what is the test of the resilience of the corporate culture? Examples abound of the good and the bad.

Continental Airlines after September 11 2001 is a great example of enlightened leadership, and a positive culture. They faced up to the realities that have been forced upon them; they took hard decisions accepted by a team who shared a culture that accepts change, because the leadership was brave, clear and honest.

GE under Jack Welch constantly lived in a culture of dynamic and positive change, again no self-delusion here. GE faced underperformance above all, honestly. No one expected to talk their way out of underperformance, but everyone also expected support if they faced up to the problems.

Perhaps the lynchpin of responsive culture is honest as well as decisive leadership. Honesty and responsiveness are the key values that are shared throughout the effective organisation. This implies the respect for individuals no matter what their allotted place in the organisation. Culture is a group property, and the group needs leadership, and the leaders in turn need support and the energy to pursue shared corporate goals.

In a culture where cynicism reigns there is unlikely to be effective response to negative influences.

Hand on Heart:
- Is your leadership, brave, clear and honest?
- Is cynicism too prevalent?

Section 3

The speed of change.

As we've discussed, the rate of change is always increasing. The problem of facing change, particularly that imposed by external factors, is that we tend to stop to analyse what has happened to us. We tend to slow down to take stock of our new condition.

If we've taken an adverse knock, we're temporarily down. What we need to do is to rejoin the race as soon as we can. To spend too much time examining our wounds is not appropriate. While we do this we are falling further and further behind our competitors and the changing conditions. We will not catch that necessary fleeting opportunity by slowing down, we'll only catch it if we are running the fastest in the competitive pack.

When trying to catch up after adverse fortune or mistakes of our own making, the avoidance of panic and muddled thinking is difficult. If we live in a culture of continuous improvement, review and action, then panic and scrambled thinking is less hard to avoid.

A sense of urgency is not the same; an organised focus allied to a sense of urgency yields concentrated team effectiveness. Special task forces may be appropriate, with clear authority, and a clear mandate understood in all levels of the business. However there is little point in appointing a special task force unless the powers that be are prepared to fully support their recommendations and actions. Despite the urgency we still need to test the hypothesis and anticipate the solution parameters.

In the face of continuous change, the manifestations of our decision-making will be unrecognisable from that which prevailed only a short time ago. Our traditional view of our culture is being stretched here. Yes we retain the values of honesty and decisive leadership, but little else can be taken for granted. Our culture map (see chapter 1 fig. 3) will have changed or at least the implied strengths and aspirations will have. The individuals in their individual organisation centres need to be constantly involved in the changing expectations and buy into the evolving aspirations of the corporation.

In times of externally imposed negative change, it's crucial that the whole organisation receives a decisive response and pitches in to help. (see; Continental Airlines.)

Hand on Heart:

- Do we react to change with decisiveness and precision?
- Would our colleagues describe our performance as sharp or dithering?

Section 4

The rock remains the same.

Changes good or bad, internally or externally imposed, leave their mark. The issue for most of us is; do we learn from them? Sadly the answer is not always in the affirmative. We have to generate a culture where we learn from our past, not just the bad things but the good things too. Continuous improvement is not a cliché, it demands a constant self examination of the body corporate at all levels. It's here that the visions of so many members of the business can be liberated to make serious positive contributions. This requires not only free expression at all levels it means a listening culture at leader level.

One of the key things that emerge from continuous improvement is the identification of contributors and by default the non-contributors. The culture of improvement yields more than just process and system improvement; it sharpens the level of personal contribution from all levels.

Getting rid of non-contributors has to be a factor in a culture firmly rooted in continuous improvement. Our culture map is always changing and the needs of the body corporate to sustain itself are not constant.

The development of talented contributors from within and the weeding out of the non-contributors, and their replacement with new and promising replacements is crucial to the survival of the corporation. These changes have to be made. They have to be made as a result of objective performance measurement derived from the basic building block of job descriptions.(see chapter 1) The underlying constants of honesty and decisiveness apply.

Continuous improvement obviously makes sense, but that must not be allowed to hide the real problems that an active culture of improvement experiences. Here is one of the great counterpoints in the sustenance of the body corporate. The enquiring intellect will see that this culture of continuous improvement is vital, but it is not enough on its own. There has to be another dimension that looks forward, into the unknown and unpredictable. It is to invite disorder into orderliness, and discontinuity into systems. It invites the re-examination of fences that might at first glance not appear to need mending. It liberates people who are encouraged to contribute and therefore fight for their ideas, and it increases the burdens of leadership and decision-making. In a place used to confidential whispering, it will be a shock to hear problems shared from the canteen to the boardroom and back again.

Continuous Improvement can encourage empire building and 'nit picking', it can be an excuse to look backwards. It can be an impediment to innovative thinking, (see red book) but even with these risks it's still an absolute necessity. Continuous Improvement is an essential part of any corporation's culture if it hopes to survive. Without it survival is impossible.

Hand on Heart:

- Can you identify the changes in behaviour and systems learned from past experience?
- Are you retaining your best colleagues and ridding yourselves of the non contributors?

Section 5

Order versus disorder, the essential opposites.

In this book we've seen a constant occurrence of opposite forces. The need to think of tomorrow; but to learn from yesterday. To be systematic and focused; but to change and evolve with alacrity. To have the building blocks of job description but to expect initiative at all levels. To liberate talent but to channel enthusiasm into a united purpose. Freedom versus discipline. Is nothing sacred in this changing scene?

We've agreed that the values of honesty and decisiveness are crucial pillars of a positive culture, and to those values we can add a third; quality. Quality not only in the products we make or the services we deliver, but also in the promises we make, and the reliability of our delivery as part of the team.

The counterpoint of the opposites are undeniable, and they are always difficult to resolve but they can be resolved if the corporate culture embraces the values of honesty, decisiveness and quality.

We have to balance the need to change against the risk of anarchy and revolution. We want focused evolution, based on continuous improvement systems, as well as a forward-looking strategy. Additionally the urgency of our requirements demand speed and initiative; versus the traditional 'let's check it all out, let's wait and see' attitudes.

These resolutions can't be confined to one level in the business. Group wide effectiveness will only come about through multi level freedom to contribute to challenges and problems. It entails a unity of purpose and a shared clarity of what the group seeks to achieve.

This cannot come about in a closed society; it can only happen in an open organisation where few, if any, secrets exist. In an open and trusting community we can expect initiative at every level. 'Just get it done' and you'll get support. That support will come easily as communication through inner and outer ring relationships pulses throughout the organisation. A culture of "Just Do It' or 'JDI', radiates confidence, because you belong and are trusted to perform.

As time marches on and the pressure builds, we have to condense the time that it takes to get things done. Put another way we have to accelerate to maintain our K1/K2 ratios. Again we meet a paradox, we have to learn our way forward rather than analyse history. Does this run counter to the idea of continuous improvement? I think it does, or rather I believe that there are dilemmas and problems that can be solved in various ways. The contrasting behaviours of learning your way forward that is less reliant on historical analysis, and learning from past experience have to co-exist. The fine judgement is applying which type of behaviour and the consequent type of analysis or action to which problem. This is one issue where top Management cannot cop out. This is where group culture has to be comfortable to live on the edge.

On the boundary of risk and trust. There will be errors but there will be many more successes.

For example many companies will analyse customer complaints in terms of what went wrong with current procedures, instead of looking at different ways to eliminate the mistakes in production or service by changing the procedure itself.

In our culture of honesty and decisiveness how we accept mistakes is very important. We need to encourage initiative and accountability. We need to be happy that if individuals make mistakes, they should say so. If they are capable and comfortable they should be encouraged to correct their own mistakes. 'If you foul up, fix it'; is a good strap line to attach to our culture definition. We can't expect courage and initiative in a risk-averse atmosphere.

Hand on Heart:

- Is your organisation as open as it might be? Are there too many secrets?
- Are you happy to address your own mistakes, do you know that you'll be encouraged to put them right?
- Are you solution or system driven?
- Does the JDI philosophy exist?

Section 6

Life is complicated.

To say that life is complicated seems something of an understatement. We have this underlying acceleration in the rate of change, an urgency that needs to be managed. It's as if we have less and less time to complete things that are more and more complicated and demanding. Dispiritingly, this is essentially true.

In an age where technical gizmos are an ever-present part of living at home and at work, it is easy to forget the essential tool of simplification, to grasp the essentials[18] and to focus on what needs change. We can simplify by using different methods rather than traditional methods. Traditional solutions are not necessarily the best ones; they survive simply because no one questions them. There is almost always a better way if you care to look. (see Red Book).

Simple is the best way, whether in defining a problem, or solution, or in the method of change. Simple ways are usually quicker, and quicker solutions take the pressure off the accelerating time frame.

Therefore if you can 'Keep it simple' and concentrate on the core of the issue or problem, you'll have more time.

Hand on Heart:

- Do you keep things simple?
- Can you simplify more of your existing procedures?

---

[18] Blanchard & Johnson –The One Minute Manager – Berkley Books

Section 7

In the face of Change.

People make up the body corporate; it is in their peculiar diversity that the uniqueness of each corporation lies. It is good that people are different and the purpose of the cultural dimension is to unify the group's intellectual output to the achievement of common goals.

No matter how wise the leadership,[19] there will always be contrasting talents deployed; hopefully appropriately, across the corporation. The placing of talent according to its strengths and shortfalls provides the value of the culture map. (See chapter 1 fig.3)

The balancing of these talent types is more than just a numbers or organisational thing. It's a very sensitive culture that allows and encourages both extremes to work effectively together and in so doing allows a culture of tension and some risk. The tolerance of the analyst and innovator side by side is essential in the balancing of past experience and innovation for the future.

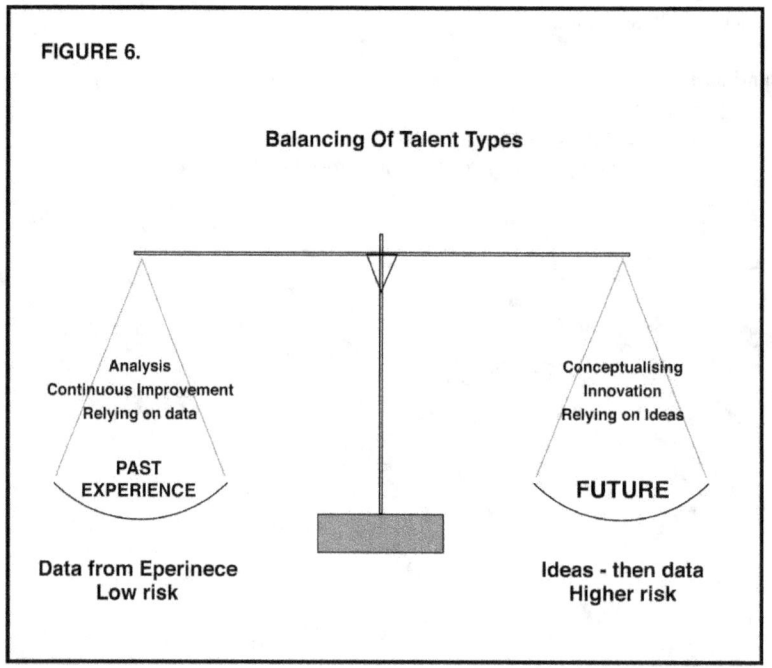

FIGURE 6.

Balancing Of Talent Types

Analysis
Continuous Improvement
Relying on data

PAST EXPERIENCE

Conceptualising
Innovation
Relying on Ideas

FUTURE

Data from Eperinece
Low risk

Ideas - then data
Higher risk

---

[19] John P Kotter – Leading Change

The balance can never be perfect; there will always be conflict at the interface between the analyst and the inventor. We must expect it, tolerate and even encourage it. For these interfaces of thinking styles are often productive sources of improvement ideas.

Those who are uncomfortable with change will be angered and aggrieved at the continuous graft of change; to them there is fear of the unknown, a demand to abandon that which they see as perfectly good systems and projects. Those who are excited by change will take an opposite view. They see past systems as an encumbrance, they find risk stimulating. The former can express their dissent by bitching and even sabotaging new initiatives. Such behaviour is not uncommon in cultures where change is brought about by external negative influences. It is very understandable.

The value of each individual to the body corporate has to be signalled time and again, as part of the appraisal process but more importantly, by the responsibility given on a day-to-day basis. The differences are recognised as having value in the continuous improvement on the one hand and on the learning from new experience on the other (see fig 6. pp 47)

The key here is to spend the energy on solutions, not on ego-defences. The solutions to transient challenges and problems can come from anywhere in the organisation. The ability to hear and balance the variety of ideas is leadership's prime responsibility. We need to include in our culture; 'the ability to listen' for without that attribute we can never be a learning organisation.

If we value our colleagues, recognise their strengths, then instead of rejecting ideas and suggestions off hand in favour of our predilections, we would do better to ask ourselves; "This is a valued colleague, why is he offering an alternative solution?" More often than we care to admit his view may well have more validity than our own.

Hand on Heart:

- Is there a ready acceptance that solutions are the goal?

- Time is not wasted, justifying defensive positions?

- Is there a culture of listening and valuing colleague ideas?

Section 8

Old strengths, new weaknesses.

One of the admitted downsides to the individually centred organisation is that if the inner ring relationships are not active then the individual can become too self-centred. It is natural for us all to defend our records of achievement, but as we discovered in Chapter 1, failure is often rooted in the success experience. It is hard to deny ourselves the satisfaction that past successes have conferred. However there is no bore like an old bore and who of us has not had a boss who continually reminisced about the 'good old days'?

It is tough but true, that the demands of the living corporation change and that inevitably the human resource must change too. Training and development of individuals has got to accommodate that aspiration column in our culture map. As its primary goal this is no 'send s/he on a five day training course every year', this is about ensuring that each individual is equipped to contribute to corporate goals effectively for as long as possible in both the individual's working life and in the corporate life itself. It's ensuring that the culture of positive change is given sustenance. It is about creating a work place where every individual has the opportunity to contribute his full measure and in so doing aspire to fulfil his/her potential. Here lies one of the few valid creators of loyalty. It's where the balance of corporate demands and individual fulfilment are given the chance to meet.

'You can't teach an old dog new tricks' has been so entrenched into corporate culture since the eighties that there seems to be a reflex view that as the pyramid of aspiration narrows and executive competition gets hard we must offload those who been instrumental in the success of this particular corporate history. It is often the case; that as the age of executives increase the greater is the demand to conform. Consequently the creative and non-conformist elements are eliminated[20] and a higher percentage of low risk takers and bureaucrats emerge as leaders not so much by merit but by conforming to the status quo culture. Fig 7. Shows that in most but not all traditional stock companies that the leadership evolves from the traditional corps of the elite. i.e. Highly educated, long service, orthodox, politically and culturally accepted model. It would be good to quote examples but probably expensive for the author. Sir John Harvey Jones in his day was an exceptional non conformist and the antithesis of the majority of leaders referred to here. These are perhaps best exemplified by those who first found themselves managing deregulated former nationalised industries. Overpaid and under achieved sums up well this all too common phenomenon.

---

[20] Getz & Drosdeck – Empowering Innovative People – Chicago:Probus Publ. Co..

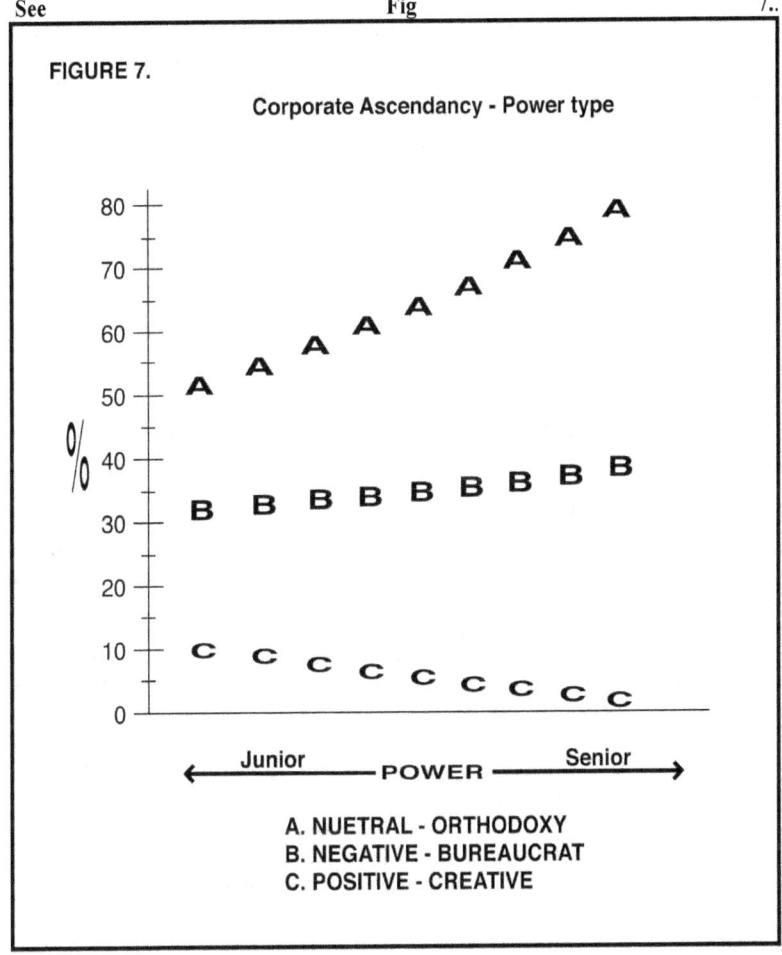

FIGURE 7.

Corporate Ascendancy - Power type

A. NUETRAL - ORTHODOXY
B. NEGATIVE - BUREAUCRAT
C. POSITIVE - CREATIVE

This type that I call orthodox; exhibit strong fixed behaviour patterns and highly disciplined and systematic responses. Imagination is not generally top of their list. Sadly these figures do not sit easily with creativity; rather they are schooled in the arts of presenting analysis and logic to shareholders who in most cases of course know little or nothing about the business. They are the arbiters of the culture of their organisations. They seldom see the need for corporate change and regeneration. Rather 'focus' is more likely to be their credo; hence the thinning out of creativity and conflict, and the nurturing of orthodoxy and continuity.

Bureaucrats therefore are more likely to have a lengthy career than the entrepreneur or the creative change agent. The odds are stacked very heavily against creative people getting to the top.

Another paradox;- As a consequence of the highly systemised responses and risk averse orthodoxy we are afraid or seemingly incapable of mobilising the corporate body's accumulated experience that may be both effective as a source of operational improvement and new ideas. It is true, we are prisoners of our own experience but that does not mean that experience is necessarily an evil. However there is subliminal belief that yesterday is the template for today. People who have been with us are therefore useful primarily for their 'experience and not for their potential. In most organisations the training and development programme is concentrated on the new entrant and becomes less and less an issue the longer the individual's service span. It seems we reward service by ensuring the self fulfilling prophesies that 'old dogs can't or won't learn new tricks.' Training and development are the key loyalty creating tools; why withhold it from our longest serving and most experienced colleagues?

This is not a defence of the elderly. Certainly individuals strengths can be outmoded, particularly if the individual has not had the opportunity to see the wider context. If long serving individuals are left to walk the treadmill of habit their talents will almost certainly become redundant.

It's easy to say that to long serving employees, 'you are no longer up to speed, it's no good doing the wrong things well.' That is self evident, but is the Corporation creating an enterprise where every individual has the opportunity to contribute his/her full maximum potential. Would we dream of not updating our computer assets? What about our human resources? Are we equipping our people to contribute to their full potential for as long as possible? Flexibility in learning new skills and developing new strengths depends as much on the organisation as on the individual. In the ever changing world, leadership has the responsibility to see that talent is liberated and sustained by the challenge of the job and the stimulus of training. Talented long service individuals need discontinuity just as much as the young trainees. Allowing talent to wither on the vine; whether it is of a twenty year old or a fifty year old, is just as much a failure of leadership, we can't claim to be a learning organisation and deny everyone the chance to be flexible and to enjoy the opportunity to learn new skills. This learning process will often demand that we do new things imperfectly.

Retraining for the individual is rather like the challenges of changing the way we think. It is huge leap from learning ideas from old data (experience), to new thinking, that creates ideas and then delivers data (new job with different skills). – This is always a risk. It recurs in every aspect of the business including the redevelopment of our people.

Hand on Heart:

- Do you offer training in new skills to longer serving employees? (not just senior Managers).
- Are you listening to those 'difficult to manage' people?
- Are there too many 'Yes men' at the top?
- Are you getting value from your team?

Section 9

Change is uncomfortable.

Even the best of organisations there are those who can't hack it. Although this book is aimed at executives, the failure to perform is not limited to the executive levels. So far we have emphasised the need for the Body Corporate to nurture its own, to develop talent, to liberate people and maximise the effective contribution from all our people through creating a learning organisation. Despite all this there will be failures at all levels. Some of these failures will be the direct result of a badly formed Culture Map, poor recruiting, but most will be individual and singular reasons that cause the individual to under-perform.

We take for granted here that these underperformers are given fair appraisals and adequate support. Some individual performances however will remain at an unacceptably low level. There can be no escaping the necessity to act here and to rid the Corporation of the underperformer. The Body Corporate has to remain fit and healthy and it cannot under any circumstances carry non-contributors. The cultural foundations of honesty and decisiveness apply as they do to all things, but especially here.

As change sweeps on[21], many if the processes and fields of operation change. It is likely that our organisation is no longer appropriate to meet the new and different demands. It is imperative we change, and that means that individuals have to change the way they work and learn new ways and new data. We may have to break down the way we did things and rebuild the way we need to do things. We may have to abandon products and systems and supersede them with products and processes that at least sustain our ratios K1/K2 and Return on Investment.

Often these changes cannot be planned with the precision we would like. Indeed there may be no opportunity to plan at all. The urgency of the need to change needs to cascade through the network of ring relationships This is often the time of 'Let's do it' and we'll see how we measure up to our solution parameters however vague they may be. Competitors are not going to hang around while we meticulously plan a detailed and planned response.

We can't catch the accelerating change by slowing down and turning inward, its time for ideas to generate new products and services, not a time for re-examining our past. The peace of routine is shattered; the disorganisation of enforced change is a reality. Under these circumstances responsiveness and flexibility are the key tools for success. We need our experienced people to be willing to risk and be proactive, not stuck in routine.

Despite the urgency to respond to externally sponsored change, the issues of quality and consistency remain our goal. The assurance of quality in all the organisation delivers is in some ways the most difficult to sustain during times of acute change.

---

[21] Price Pratchett – Culture Shift

Some people will see their guardianship of quality standards as a reason to fight against change; others will see the pressures of ever more urgent demands as compromising. These people are right.

Furthermore we need them, they are right to guard against compromising quality, but they should also be comfortable in a team where these challenges and risks are overcome. These people are the abrasive element in the mill of change. They do not resist change but they are a consistent reminder that risk wherever possible should be limited as a consequence of evolutionary change rather than cavalier revolutionary change. Those who seek to move and drive change forward need to value the guardian of the key values of quality. This is constructive conflict, conflict that we should be happy to live with.

These issues of conflict, of analysis versus ideas, of the need for speedy change versus the need to sustain absolute quality, the need to do things well but to have a learning and flexible workforce, the need to train and develop the experienced as well as the new entrants hold enormous challenges at the personal level throughout the organisation.

We all have a tendency to protect our status and our field of responsibility. Indeed pride and the defence of our own record are integral parts of a balanced psyche. It is only in the most secure environments that we will find it possible to escape our defensive protectionism.

Without the concept of the individually centred organisation and the blueprint of the constantly updated Culture Map, the self-protection culture is almost bound to prevail. In such an environment the idea of improving organisational effectiveness becomes subordinate to self-protection and self-preservation. Corporate unity is no longer a viable principle.

Individuals have to be comfortable and secure to be able to think beyond 'me' issues. The Body Corporate has to have running through its culture the ideas that it's the customer who decides the future, and it's the competitors who want to eat our lunch. Each member and team needs to keep these tenets central to all their decisions and actions.

Hand on Heart:

- Does everyone serve the customer and fear the competitor?

- Is conflict stamped out or productively resolved?

- Does quality underpin everything, even change initiatives?

Section 10

Members of the Body Corporate.

Apart from our personal ambition and need to earn a living most of us like to belong. Many of us not only like to belong but need to belong, to be part of a social group that shares a purpose and manifests that purpose through the group's corporate effort. This cultural need to belong has at its centre an equation that attempts the almost impossible balance between the group and individual goals.

We've already examined some of these conflicts and it is easy to see that resolution of these conflicts is seldom absolute. The task of leadership includes making belonging easy. It is perhaps easier to define what belonging does not demand rather than what it does.

An effective member of the Body Corporate does not give loyalty to the glories of things past. The notion of a sort of Corporate Imperialism where old conquests owe us a living is a recipe for an early demise. Belonging must require the desire to contribute and assisting the team to achieve future goals. This frequently requires the breaking of traditional chains and customs. Defending the past will not protect us from the slings and arrows that future may direct at us. If we live in a corporation where the culture is made up of selfish defences, worship of past glories and changes built solely on past experience, we won't be there for the long haul. This Corporate Body is too sick to survive into much of a future..

So what should it be like to belong to a healthy Corporation? In some ways effective team membership carries with it the iconoclastic dimension of constant impatience and an urgent desire to move forward; frequently into uncharted waters.

Firstly it's not an easy place to work, problems and conflict will abound, the difference is that the attitudes that prevail will be looking for positive solutions. You will be encouraged to contribute and to take prime responsibilities. If you don't succeed then help will be at hand. If you make a mistake you'll be encouraged to fix it. Your ring relationships will be open and constructive sharing goals and tasks as and when appropriate. As a group you will look for opportunity, there will be a 'Can do' attitude. When a job is done you'll be encouraged to seek another.

There will be stress, but there will be optimism too. There will be expectancy and an eagerness for tomorrow. There will be a good deal of humour. You will laugh a lot, agonise a lot. But most nights you'll go home happy that you made a contribution. You'll understand that fixers are better than blamers, and that you are not afraid to propose solutions to problems, you'll know how to say 'I fouled up. I'll try and put it right'. You'll listen to your colleagues new or old and you'll be prepared to learn. You'll have the courage to think of new ideas and to test them. Each day you'll answer the questions; "How did I contribute to changes for the better?' and "What did I learn today?

Hand on Heart:

- Do you live on past glories, and yearn for the 'Good old days'?

- Are you focused on tomorrow?

- Do you look to future challenges with an open mind?

- Is there a pride, about working in your Corporation?

The Red Book

Rejuvenation and longevity

Chapter1

Sustaining Success.

Section 1.

Waiting for what?

Corporate life is tough and getting tougher. The speed of information flow, a highly competitive deflationary environment and complicated ethical issues are all likely to accelerate change even faster. Survival from day to day is hard enough, full of contrary influences and impossible opposites. Perhaps it is not surprising that in such a hostile environment few Companies survive and grow over any significant time span.

Most of the corporate failures[22] (corporate malfeasance excepted.) are brought about by the pre-occupation with the defence of old and outdated ideas and products. This inability to escape from the nostalgia of former glory and success is the single biggest cause of corporate decline.

It's not so much that the old products or processes are wrong, they are not. It's the pre-occupation with breathing life into an out-dated idea that's bad. We ought to exspend our energy on tomorrow's successes. We have to remember that we need to replace and eventually abandon practices and products that no longer maintain our K1/K" or ROCE.

The snag is that we are so busy practising the difficulties of day to day management that it's hard to recognise the slide from success to moderation to failure[23]. **(see fig.8)**

---

[22] Donald Sull – Revival of the fittest
[23] Sydney Finklestein – Why Smart Executives fail.

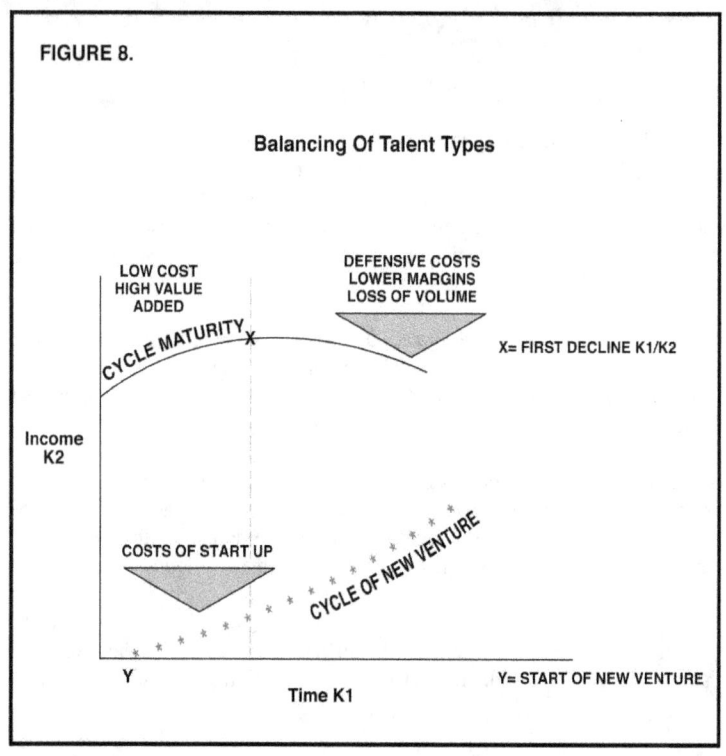

FIGURE 8.

Balancing Of Talent Types

It is important to know that we are talking 'sins of omission' not sins of commission. It's what we don't do to ensure growth that is the missing link. It is the growth factor that is the best defence against take-over or atrophy. When the Body Corporate ceases to grow then stagnation leads to defensive strategies that usually lead to 'downsizing' and eventual collapse. The lower area of figure 8 marked 'x' shows the negative costs associated with static or defensive strategies. Put at its simplest 'it costs money, when the company ceases to grow.' Of course growth costs as well; the issue of absolute measurement is the continual growth of K1/K2 and sustenance of ROCE.

What is it then, which is missing? We've come a long way, we've been successful, and we know our success formula. "Don't change that which doesn't need fixing." Is the cry from employees and analysts alike. But they're wrong; we know they're wrong if we look at history. If we are a good 'Blue Book' operator it's not enough, because the changing markets will sooner or later inhibit our growth and the consequences are inevitable.

Acquisitions are the quick road to growth, although the productivity of most acquisitions is seldom equal to internally generated new ventures. Many acquisitions fail to deliver simply because the cultural synergies do not work.

There have been many examples of acquisitions and take overs from virtually every sector from the motor industry to natural resources, there are hosts of examples. They do not work, principally because the Acquirer is unable to accept the Acquired as an equal. The acquired are virtually always treated as subordinate and not surprisingly many of the pre-acquisition virtues are eroded. Even in so called friendly mergers there are strong cultural strictures that inhibit real integration of two corporate bodies with disparate histories. Few companies involved in acquisitive strategies pay enough attention to this aspect and all too often pay the price.

The acquisition route to growth is often a poor strategy in that the targets are either too high priced if they're still growing, or alternatively passed their prime and have a lot of disgruntled shareholders who will support a hostile bid. In both cases the Acquirer has an enormous difficulty in assimilating the new acquisition that requires a high degree of asset sweating, or imposing cost saving and downsizing that squeezes out any positive energy. There has been much inventive accounting to fog these issues and after three years even the most dogged analyst is bamboozled into believing that "market conditions have not been favourable but the Acquirer is satisfied with the acquisition that has yielded important market synergies, cost savings etc. etc." It is rare indeed that an acquisition is an unqualified success.

Cash Mountains that are the product of a successful era, tempt many into the acquisitive mode, however there is a valid view that if we consider income as the food of the Body Corporate, squirreling away large quantities of it, is unproductive; more should have been geared into growth strategies along the way. Cash Mountains to some are a symbol of atrophy and as such a symptom of an ailing enterprise. In the famous case of GE Marconi the urge to spend the cash mountain all but sank what was once a great corporation.

I am not being dismissive of an acquisitive strategy, I'm pointing out that few succeed and that this is fraught with danger. The energy required to launch a successful hostile bid is huge and costly, sapping up resources and cash at almost unimaginable rates.

Outside the acquisitive route, what are the other ways to growth? Opportunity may well knock. Can we borrow or steal ideas from others? Can we imitate successful competitors? We can use outside agencies to help us. Surely if we have an excellent continuous improvement culture we will generate lots of productivity improvements. What else will rejuvenate the prospects for the future?

The Red Book takes us beyond the 'learning corporation' and leads to the 'Creative Corporation.' This is the only way to attain rejuvenation and continual growth.

Hand on Heart:

- Are you planning the next corporate move as well as enjoying corporate success?

Section 2

Creativity, recognising the need?

Many and erudite are those who have written about 'Creativity'. I have been a fan of Dr Edward de Bono for many years and would heartily recommend his books on the subject. The message that he teaches amongst others is that techniques of creative behaviour can be learned. I endorse this view and would go further; I believe that a corporation that does not actively encourage creative training as part of their management development programme is unlikely to survive in the longer term.

Creativity explains de Bono depends on our ability to escape from traditional ways of thinking. He states that lateral thinking depends heavily on discontinuity and the breaking up of conditioning patterns that are reinforced by traditional educational and business mores. This is not the only way to creative thinking and development, but it is central to the concepts that define creativity, the implications being that we are seeking something that has never been done before, a new way, a new product. The idea of creativity goes beyond evolution, it implies the acceptance of revolutionary ideas.

Yet throughout the 'Blue Book' there's been the constant exhortation to stick to evolution rather than revolution. We are close to another opposite here, and indeed the creative corporation operates closer, as it were, to the revolutionary limit than relying entirely on continuous improvement and the evolutionary drive that results from that foundation. Evolutionary development will sustain cycle 1 in figure 9 but it is unlikely to stimulate the initiative for the new cycles for completely new products or services in cycles 2 & 3 etc..

Cycle 1 of course may be many years; it would be unreasonable to expect the founder of a new business to abandon enthusiasm for his founding 'idea' and immediately to set out to have another. However the time always comes when that first idea shows signs of redundancy, and usually we see the need to change too late. As we stated earlier there are costs associated with defensive strategies and there are costs associated with start-ups. Too late in the piece and we find ourselves heavily committed to defence, even downsizing, it's then very much harder to invest in development for new ideas for products and services. Many corporations find themselves in this very uncomfortable dilemma. The Market is often unsympathetic to requests for extra equity capital for a company apparently and very probably passed its best.

In the 'Blue Book'; 'watch the clocks' in section 2 Chapter 1, refers to the many clocks, from the calendar to market seasons and not least to the life rhythms of the corporation. However as the Corporation gets bigger it gets harder to recognise the changes, even harder to predict balanced maturity for example.

Balanced maturity I would define as the point (x) in fig.8. It's where the rate of acceleration of K1/K2 begins to decline. The reasons for this decline may be manifold and our every day Blue Book team will manage to mitigate and prolong the cycle life. The beginning of the end calls for resources to be allocated to the new beginning. At this point we are carrying least cost and can afford to invest into creative research; we can attach more emphasis to revolution than our day to day evolution.

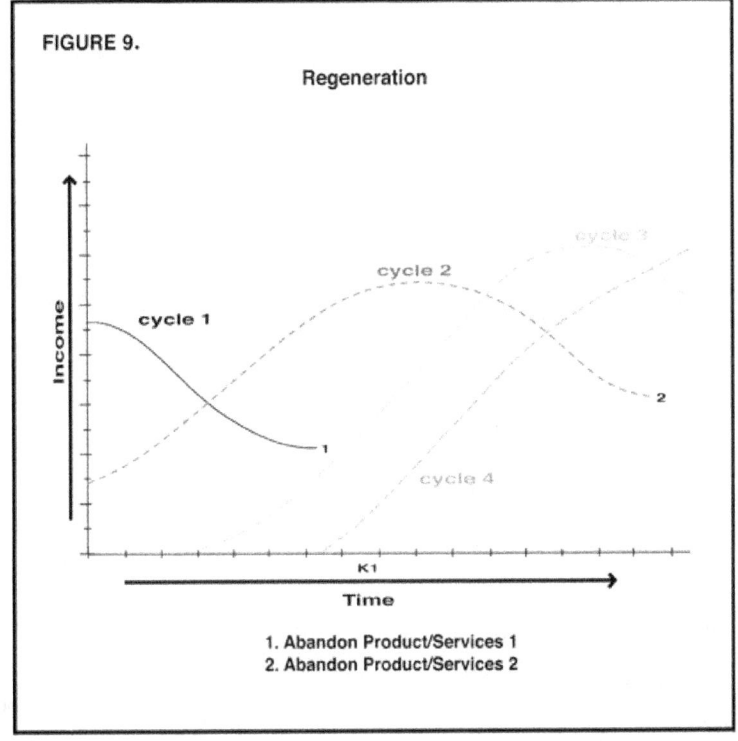

FIGURE 9.

Regeneration

cycle 3

cycle 2

cycle 1

Income

1

2

cycle 4

K1

Time

1. Abandon Product/Services 1
2. Abandon Product/Services 2

You will, I hope, remember that it is natural to blame bad or negative events to 'other' than our selves. The recognition of the deceleration of the K1/K2 performance is often not recognised for what it is; namely the early signs of maturation of the business cycle. We ascribe the slowdown to all sorts of reasons and it's easy to support these speculations that we are the victims of external negative forces. This is a cop out. We have to recognise that if we are in the wrong place at the wrong time, we had better do something to make sure we change our position for 'new time and place'. Creative thinking about what is our next move in terms of repositioning has to go further than just tinkering with the business. If it doesn't, then before we know it we're thrust into an expensive defensive strategy; fighting the market share war. In so doing we're pressuring out our ability to create new ideas test new hypotheses, we're succumbing to overpowering short term thinking.

Once we learn to recognise our own accountability to create change then we're on our way to tomorrow's challenges. We will be much better equipped to manage new ideas; indeed we will sense the imperative to create them.

Hand on Heart:

- Is your K1/K2 still improving?

- Is your K1/K2 slowing?

- What positive moves can be made to improve?

- Can you resist a first move to cut back?

Section 3

Creative people.

Creativity is good. After all God created man, we admire creative artists and in a way artists are the consummate creative marketers. From Beethoven to the Beetles from Shakespeare to Steven King. These creative minds have produced works unequalled by any other composer of their genre. Their products are unique. Each time they pen a piece of music, or poetry or prose they reach to ideas that are truly original 'creations'. Their success is enduring and they remain market leaders.

Ask any manager if he is a creative being and he will reply, "Yes I think I have some creative talent". It's rather like asking someone, "Are you a good human being?" The answer will almost certainly affirm some degree of 'goodness', whatever that means.

In this world of almost universal admiration for creativity, surely creative behaviour and processes are easily accepted and practiced. In corporate society creative skills are admired and encouraged. Sadly this is not so. Why?

Here is another mighty opposite, creativity is good, but creativity is discouraged, misunderstood and mistrusted. Even more bizarrely most of us are not aware of this paradox. Most people in corporate life really believe that they are creative, open minded and receptive to new ideas. Few of us are.

Creative people are not people set apart, eccentrically musing in inventors' dens. They are like you and me, their difference lies in their ability to accommodate the disconnected ideas. They are more likely to have the habit of living in 'tomorrow' or sometimes they can be obsessively engaged in the pursuit of goals that are rarely shared with others. However obsessive behaviour is true of all ambitious people. The only difference lies in our perception of normality, or our ability to at least have sympathy with the object of the obsession, the idea.. It is perfectly all right for the finance Director to worry obsessively about financial results, we can understand this. The only difference with the creative obsession is that we seldom understand the new idea.

From my own experience of managing creative people, they tend to be loners unless they are in a creative team with composite goals. These teams are very productive if they are insulated from the straight jacket of routine. . Creative people tend to be disinterested in the rules, roles and tasks of other people; they are often not 'team players' in the ordinary sense of the words. The key issue must be to ensure that the connection between the creative and the corporate is always alive and relevant. It is no use having undisciplined creative teams becoming disconnected from corporate goals.

The interface between the creative teams and the corporate main stream may not be drawn from the creative team itself. What is needed is a linkman that is good listener and articulate enough to translate the hypothesis into sympathetic corporate ears. To sell the new ideas to the backers who matter and make the decisions.

There are degrees of creative ability from Beethoven to Bob Hope; neither would have been a good man to have around in a nuclear power plant. The great comedians are a fine example of creative genius. They get their laughs from constantly delivering the unexpected. Many are, I understand almost impossible to live with; because they are so concerned with discontinuity that they become entirely disconnected themselves. Many highly creative artists in private life become depressed in their disconnected worlds and frequently break down in one way or another. These creative artists whether they are painters, musicians, writers or comedians, to name but a few, have a much higher average depression rate and between them exhibit a much higher degree of disconnection and dysfunctional behaviour. It has been postulated[24] that the constant drive to find new expression in whatever the art is for many an obsession without end, or satisfactory conclusion. Examples again are legion, from Beethoven, Tony Hancock, to Dylan Thomas.

Are we talking about the same sort of people here? In some senses we are, after all creators are in the business of discontinuity and invention. Yet clearly there are different examples of creative flair that we find in invention, and yet there is another kind of talent that translates invention into product. There is yet another type of deductive creative flair based on highly specialised data in science and technology. Academic learning is seldom creative in itself; in fact the opposite is true. It is only when the scientist risks those leaps into the unknown that the creative act is delivered, yet to be tested against its hypothesis.

Here is another dilemma; for our formal education as experienced by the majority is a system that denies the virtue of discontinuity in thinking and discourages new ideas as yet unproven. Academic examinations after all demand you cram as many pieces of data as you can and then regurgitate this data to prove you know the subject. This is not the forum for creative thinking, - you must be right to succeed. Postulating new ideas will certainly, in most formative academic theatres, be positively discouraged. Education above all is based on learning and absorbing existing knowledge. Today this is more and more reinforced with younger scholars being challenged by multiple choice answers in examination papers. This is good but it is not good in the forming of creative minds. This trend stamps out even more emphatically the options for laterally thought out options. Creativity has little relevance in secondary school or early university education. Of all the countries in the world only a few have embraced the teaching of creative skills. Australia is a shining example.

On the scale of natural creative flare there are a wide range of abilities; many potentially creative people have their creative talent educated out of them. Some recognise the antipathy that creative behaviour generates and suppress the talent, others don't have it. Certain industries such as banking and insurance are built on risk aversion and statistical or actuarial foundations, not much room for creativity here. This is changing following the entrepreneurial example of the growth in Silicone

---

[24] Hersham –The Key to Genius: Manic depression and the creative life – Prometheus 1988

valley, yet bankers still want to lend where there is security, creative initiatives are seldom strong from the banks. Certainly in the UK high street banks have an appalling reputation as supporters of new enterprise, almost entirely because average Bank Mangers are discouraged to use any creative scope and are entirely concerned with avoidance of risk. The consequence for the UK economy in the 70's and 80's was a massive 'Brain Drain' from the UK to the USA where venture capital companies are still less risk averse. This has changed, though UK venture Capital is still used primarily in the salvage game.

If we accept the need to regenerate and rejuvenate the Body Corporate, then we have to accept the necessity of harnessing creative ability and power into the enterprise. To move from the idea to the practice is immensely difficult. To incorporate ideas that are disconnected and laterally developed into an organisation that is built on the logical exploitation of a set of ideas usually derived (successfully) from one founding idea; is contrary to horizontal and logical thinking and hence the prevailing culture. It flies in the face of logic, invites disruption, is unpredictable, and endangers the status quo. No wonder we go into denial.

There is little doubt that we all have some creative talent, just as we've all some goodness, but few have the degree of creative drive that is strong enough to make a difference. The majority of us are good at processing data and thinking logically which is vital to keep the enterprise alive, logical thinking is the prevalent method of processing data and it must remain so. That is another reason why creative processes are so difficult to integrate. No organisation can go into an entirely lateral thinking anarchy, but equally if we're locked into the routine of logical thinking it's hard to escape into a lateral mode when a step change is required.

As always it's the Human resource that makes or breaks the proposition, which is to have logical and lateral thinking talents productively integrated. Every organisation needs an ordered logical core but to rejuvenate it must have access to creative energy from a source that by definition is less ordered. The organisation has to be leavened with creative people; these people must be purposely acquired, and recognised for what they are. They must be identified in our culture map. They need to come from many disciplines and contribute in many areas. These people are not freaks they are just a little different from the less creative colleagues.

These creative people are not geniuses, they're people who have sustained a curiosity and unorthodox (as we see it) way of looking at routine problems. Their core skills are measured just as every other member of the corporation. We are looking to them for qualities that will almost certainly include quick humour, something akin to a lack of concentration, they need challenge, perhaps manifested by an apparent unstable or varied career record. They are easily bored and move on more than the average. So we're looking for core competence plus a curiosity and apparently less focused view of life in general. Yet most importantly we're looking for an enthusiast who seeks the opportunity for self-expression. What's created the apparent instability in his or her record is often the result of the frustrations at being constrained, muzzled and not challenged. We are not looking for a conformist or a yes man we are looking for a manageable antithesis.

There are difficulties in balancing the needs of discipline and freedom, the corporate plan and the room for self-expression, the order of continuous improvement versus the risks of unproven ventures. Discipline versus creative disorder.

Do we have the courage to acknowledge the need for these unorthodox people and the need for change? Do we have the leadership and the culture to tolerate a deliberately introduced degree of disorder?

Earlier in the Blue Book we talked of giving individuals the chance to lead peer group (inner group relations) to solve problems, thus often negating a series of unproductive meetings. Likewise we need to get teams led by creative people who select their own teams to look at problem solving and new venture development. Later we will discuss new venture development in more depth.

Allowing, even encouraging everyone in the organisation to have room for self expression will in any event liberate a generally more creative atmosphere. There's no agenda here to separate the creative recruits from the 'others', on the contrary we are encouraging the enthusiasm for self-expression whether lateral or logical. What is important is that the logical and lateral arguments are given equal opportunity. More often than not it will be easier for the group to accept logical argument than lateral thinking. The reason is obvious we have spent our lives and more particularly our education making yes/no judgements based on known data.[25] There needs to be a strong infusion of training and development for the entire organisation if they are to tolerate and accept the value of laterally induced ideas as opposed to the logical ones. As said earlier logical arguments are accepted because they're logical, not because they are the best alternative.

What we're seeking to achieve is a creative Body Corporate where all the members are capable of living in a hybrid culture where individual strengths are recognised; be they based on logical or lateral types of thinking. Even the orthodox administrator has to recognise that laterally developed ideas have to be given air time. Likewise the creatives amongst us must accept the logical challenge. All the hypotheses need to stand equal examination and qualification. If there is conflict we need a culture that resolves that conflict with tolerance and a strong belief that all the ideas were given an honest and fair hearing. Neither creative people nor those who are deeply entrenched in the status quo are good at this and are prone to close minded defences of their ideas; it's as well to be aware of this. Creative people, just like the rest of us sulk if their ideas are rejected or even challenged, like us all they are deeply committed to their idea. Belief and pride in ideas generates emotional defence when challenged, under these conditions people are apt to dig defensive trenches; leadership is required to resolve these issues.

Hand on Heart:

- Is your organisation leavened with creative people?

---

[25] de Bono – Lateral thinking for Managers – McGraw-Hill

- Are these people valued and listened to?

- Is management willing to balance the arguments and resolve the inevitable conflicts?

Section 4

The Challenges of Creativity.

The 'Mega' Corporation was a Blue Chip Corporation that had been one of the most successful brands in the world. However their philosophy was focus, so they did, and reinforced the brand time and time again. The brand became omni-present but market growth began to decrease since they'd come close to the practical limit of market penetration. Mega had become extremely rich.

A defensive strategy of acquisition was eventually alighted upon. The acquisitions were treated to the brand reinforcement game that in some instances was entirely an unnecessary expense. (These acquired companies had a well established brands into very discrete market segments and were very close to their customers.) Each of the acquired companies was passed its most expansive phase. However 'focus' was to be the answer and of course; better brand management. One by one the acquired companies diluted the parent company's profits.

Then the CEO discovered creativity, so he appointed a Director of Creativity (not important enough to sit on the main Board.). He chose for the job an IT oriented person who was as single minded as could be, albeit he fitted the picture of the eccentric academic. There was no discernable change in company direction.

In took ten years from their ascendancy as a world brand leader to a take-over by an even bigger brand leader in an associated industry. The companies that had been so recently acquired as a defence were broken up and sold.

An apocryphal tale, but a common one: It shows that even well placed and wealthy corporations have little or no idea about the real meaning of creative initiative. They were quite unable to escape from their past successes. They were bankrupt when it came to initiating new ideas, they could only re-work old ones. Thousands of jobs and millions of pounds were swallowed up and lost for ever. The CEO moved on with a multi-million package to numerous executive and non-executive roles to share his skills of brand management and his philosophy of 'focus'.

The above example is not that unusual and illustrates extremely well the real fear of change even in powerful and wealthy corporations. 20/20 hindsight vision is of course easy, but nevertheless this story has been repeated time and again in recent years in industries that range from automobiles to the oil business to electronics. Even after the take- over of quite massive billion dollar enterprises there tends to be no criticism of the managements; as shareholders of the acquired pocket their profits and move onto another 'opportunities' The waste is immense, particularly when in most cases the creative talent to grow and regenerate these corporations existed, but was not allowed to take hold.

This waste is all the more tragic in that years of experience, entrepreneurial excellence, and the 'traditions' of invention are discarded and lost for ever. There are far too many forty to fifty year old early-retired but frustrated technologists, marketers and entrepreneurs cast on the scrap heap because leadership has been afraid of liberating non conventional creative change.

The first challenge of Managers who are serious about rejuvenating their corporate charges is to audit the ideas that already exist. Not an audit that counts and records, an audit that discovers and listens to members of the corporations who have 'ideas'. Ideas not based on past experience but not excluding them either. We talk of the learning organisation evolving into a creative organisation; here is the first challenge.

Although we have discussed discontinuity and leaps into the unknown, creativity is a much more down to earth tool than the 'Eureka' syndrome. Creativity can be applied in a disciplined fashion as long as the culture is right. We have to change from the first thought negative reactions to the new hypotheses: "Why can't we....?"

If we live with creativity as an integral part of our corporate culture, we could suspend our reflex negative judgement. If we employ intelligent colleagues we ought to be able, to give air time to their ideas.

Disciplined creativity relies upon the acceptance of the need to change and the recognition of our own corporate strengths and weaknesses. It is wise to have these views corroborated by an objective outside agency. Strengths and weaknesses should be expressed in terms of markets, skills, technology, people and liquidity. Seldom can a weakness be the valid base for creative initiative, the cause of that weakness is often simply habit. A simple change can sometimes eliminate weaknesses by repositioning our assumptions. (for example – A car dealer may blame his supplier for falling sales. Perhaps this fall in sales is due to his locale rather than the marketing support from his car provider. His dominant idea has been that marketing support makes the difference. However demographic changes have contributed to the decline. This has happened gradually but the entrenched dominant idea has not changed.) It is impossible to break even this simple dominant idea without creative input, however modest the degree of creativity.

An honest examination of our existing assumptions, our strengths, harnessing the attributes of our successes is vital if we are to see ways of using them in different ways. We need to challenge our first phase thinking where all these assumptions lie. Here lies the repeating creative challenge; to rigorously question and challenge the status quo. Such challenges deserve a forum where imaginative and lateral ideas are given air. It's a place where 'What if?' is applied to existing assumptions and projected to the future. It's a place where ideas are provoked and not judged.- Not yet; ideas are not allowed to be strangled at birth, but given time to be developed and nurtured. Most of all this is a place where ideas come first, and these ideas generate data not the other way around.[26] So this is the second challenge; to generate practical

---

[26] de Bono – Lateral Thinking for managers – McGraw-Hill

ideas that utilise the corporate strengths to expand our products, process capability, skills and services into new arenas.

Once we have an effective forum, firmly based on 'future' developments, then ideas will come. Some will be hopeless, some brilliant and many useful. The second challenge is to filter these ideas and to use them effectively. In this situation the selection of an idea is a decision. However a decision is not a decision until it is acted upon. (see Blue Book.) There is an additional challenge in the sensitive handling of ideas that are not to be used. Once more the basic tenets of our leadership ethics come into play; decisiveness and honesty.

How to innovate and minimise risk?

- Firstly; the innovation should introduce only one dimension of radical change at a time, e.g. you are skilled in manufacturing steel widgets to the boat building industry. You can change the product, the material, the method of manufacture or the customer base. But to minimise risk you will change only one at a time

- Secondly; you will prototype to a limited field within a planned timescale.

- Thirdly; you will make one person the champion, who will fight the difficulties of change that are bound to arise.

The most common failures are:

- Trying to change too much at once.

- Trying to introduce it too quickly and too widely.

- Giving up too early.

- Giving up too late

- No champion.

Hand on Heart:

- Do you systemise your internally driven new venture programme?

- Do you review new venture projects within predetermined time fences?

- If you are hell bent on acquisition, have you a plan to integrate the cultures?

Chapter 2

Regeneration

Section 1

Making creativity work..

In the heady climate of creative adventure it is important to remember that it is much easier to regenerate from a healthy body corporate than an ailing one. The Body Corporate has a limited energy that has to be channelled efficiently into sustaining and growing K1/K2 or ROCE and at the same time keeping resources in reserve for rejuvenation and regeneration. The balancing of these energy outputs is difficult, there is risk here, for creative ideas have no value in themselves. Sometimes they do not deliver effective and positive results. There is no guarantee that all, or indeed any of our creative initiatives will succeed.

The testing and evaluation of projected result parameters is a crucial discipline that has to co-exist with a creative environment. New ideas have to be championed, and that championing has to be spirited and aggressive if new ideas have any chance of seeing the light of day. Equally the objective testing of new hypothesis has to be powerful and disciplined. Although this questioning and testing of hypothesis is crucial it must be seen to be open minded and fair. Finding grounds for rejecting new ideas is dangerously easy and can be made convincing to the majority (excluding the champion) because the rebuttal will usually be based on existing assumptions.

Each culture[27] as it matures gathers dominant ideas that constantly reinforce past success and the ingrained habits that govern its current behaviour. These dominant ideas can put the company into a rigid mind-set that precludes creative initiative. These dominant ideas condition existing assumptions. There are many examples of this, Marconi's demise comes to mind, BMW's acquisition of Rover is another. Regrettably there are many instances of these types of errors brought about by one dominant idea. Alternatively; the great successes of the Twentieth century that illustrate an escape from dominant ideas include General Electric, and 3M.

When new ideas are challenged, the grounds for rebuttal must be qualified with a statement of the underlying assumptions. These may well prove irrelevant. This is a major obstacle to creative progress; more good ideas are scrapped because they are rejected on the grounds of existing positions. To suspend our judgement and put aside theses presumptions is very difficult. It is difficult because of the deeply engrained logical thinking systems that we all possess. We have to escape from the alternatives of Yes or No and become much more comfortable using, What if? Or even Po, neither yes nor no. Of all the genius that is De Bono this is perhaps the simplest and most brilliant tool that he ever invented. (see: De Bono Lateral Thinking.)

The Champion of new ideas there must be not only be intelligent and have the necessary technical excellence, but also have ample emotional drive. Without it a Champion is unlikely to win his cause. In some ways the terms 'spirit', 'emotions', and 'courage', are strangers to the business of business, but we all know that these

---

[27] Birch & Clegg – Imagination Engineering –(Challenging assumptions)

qualities are crucial to creating meaningful change. Whilst we are perhaps more comfortable with 'imagination', firing up, what little of this there is in the average corporate headquarters, demands courage and drive in spades. The new idea Champion is of no use without the emotional commitment to make new ideas into a reality.

Figure 10. Emotional output.

FIGURE 10.

Emotional Output of Concept Champion

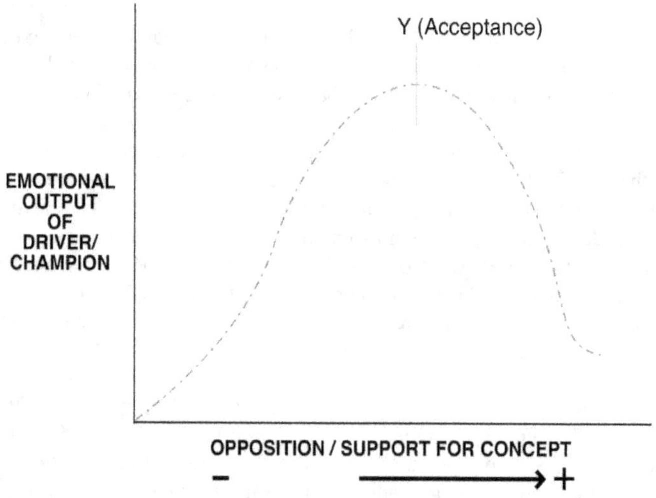

Y (Acceptance)

EMOTIONAL OUTPUT OF DRIVER/ CHAMPION

OPPOSITION / SUPPORT FOR CONCEPT

In fig 10 we can see that the originator of the idea or the champion of the new concept puts in a huge amount of emotional energy into the promotion of his or her idea. The emotional content of energy gets higher as does commitment, until support is generated through others. Often the originator can loose much of his/her emotional drive at this stage and characteristically in some cases be quite prepared to abandon all further involvement with the development of the idea. For these people, the challenge is to win over others to acceptance the new idea. Once this is done they are quite happy to walk away. These types of people make excellent New Venture Champions, although the dangers and risks associated with this behaviour are obvious. High emotional energy can lead to distortion of the true idea; emotional commitment can move the originator away from the solution parameters and even to exaggerate results of prototype evaluation.

In case you think I am painting a picture of an anarchic mad house full of over-wrought inventors, I am not[28]. However we need to recognise that these emotional conflicts and energies exist. Perhaps not as part of the main agenda, they are not, nor should they be the dominant driving force. They are not the hard lines of the foundation drawing or even the block colours that characterise the subject. But they are important and an essential part of the make up of a creative enterprise. We are used to caring for our fellows, caring for assets but we have to care for ideas as well. The acceptance of new ideas and creative insight defines the positive humour of the body corporate. Without it the corporate culture is without its dreams.

Having become aware of the ideas that already exist and encouraging the generation of new ones; we have to accept that this will lead to much livelier enterprise with a good deal more challenge and conflict. We cannot simply impose these conditions on an unprepared existing stable and successful company, for in all likelihood the creative initiative would be extinguished within a short time.

Corporate leadership has to take stock and answer the questions;
Hand on Heart:

- Do we tolerate, welcome or encourage new ideas?

- Do the people in this organisation understand the importance of new ideas?

- What do you need to do to prepare the way to getting positive answers to all these questions?

---

[28] John J Kao - Managing Creativity – Prentice Hall 1991

Section 2

Training and Development

The members of the Corporation will not accept a change as radical as this without substantial training support. The first area is the conditioning of attitudes and the recognition therein of the different types and qualities of talent that need to co-exist productively. As mentioned earlier we have to train our people into the techniques of creative thinking whether they are non-creative, moderately creative or very creative. What is important is that every one is in a position to understand[29] the process and recognise that new laterally evolved ideas have to be treated differently from vertically developed ones based on existing data.

Only when there is a general awareness of these needs will new ideas be tolerated and given any sort of chance to develop. Even in the most enlightened creative enterprise the pressures of day to day management will inevitably crowd out all but the most powerful ideas, success requires talented idea champions who have substantial inter-personal skills as well as the technical ability sets to support the idea cogently.

We are redrawing the Culture map.

Hand on Heart:

- Has everyone in your company been exposed to training on creativity?

---

[29] Michael Michaelko – Cracking Creativity – Ten Speed Press 1998
Parnes Noller & Biondi – Guide to Creative Action- Scribner

Section 3

Creativity Champions

Choosing the right champion to carry the creative banner and providing the appropriate forum for new initiatives is obviously of vital importance. Assuming that the corporate training and development has been completed then what sort of person and what sort of position are we talking about?

The majority of corporations are small, under $5 million, and the majority of these have under a hundred employees. No matter if it's a $10 billion or a small start up, the New Ideas Champion has to be in a position to be heard at all levels in the business and have the committed support of the leadership, be it the Board of Directors or the Proprietor.

The Champion must command respect at all levels and have the 'street credibility' in the factory, the Board room and in the market place.

The Champion has to have a high degree of interpersonal skill to face and resolve conflict positively. S/He has to articulate well in all forms of communication.

The Champion has to have enormous energy and considerable qualities of leadership.

The Champion does not have to be highly technically qualified in any particular discipline although a person with the talents described will have acquired a strong track record in his/her chosen field. To some extent a healthy scepticism about existing core values and an innocence of existing dominant ideas is desirable.

This job will give the job holder access to the whole of the corporation, absolute support and trust must be taken as read. In the right cultural environment this is a job for a potential CEO. In the wrong culture this job will either be irrelevant and a road to obscurity or the beginning of the end of a promising career. The Champion requires courage to face risk as almost routine!

For a leadership that cares to think about the corporation's long term future this appointment may come from many levels. It would be useful to consider the appropriate profile most likely to succeed. Those who appoint too junior a candidate should not expect good results since the incumbent is unlikely to have the appropriate gravitas. Too mature a candidate is unlikely to have the flexibility to reach all levels easily. There are of course exceptions. These are not rules; they are an indication of the profile most likely to succeed. The Seniority of this appointment might well be a new Board appointment in a larger Corporation, i.e. Director of New ventures, but care must be taken to ensure that such a senior appointment does not pressurise the incumbent into conforming with the dominating culture.

The fig 8 below outlines a possible job description for a 'New Venturer' within the corporation. Note that the main purpose of the job is to generate new ventures from within corporate resources. This means expanding on the strongest attributes of the company's marketing, process or product/service base. Simply put, the question is can we expand our business by creating new markets for the same products, new products for the same markets, new products from the same processes? We are expanding into new areas but with the risk minimised because at least two thirds of our product/process/market pyramid base is preserved in any one new venture.

The most creative leap is probably using existing technologies or processes into other markets. For example there was a company that manufacture high temperature insulators for the metallurgical industries. That technology could and was introduced into a number of alternative markets using high temperature insulators and materials. Examples are to the ceramics and pottery industries, even the domestic artificial gas flame hearth market the aeronautics market and the aerospace markets. The attributes of the technology were relatively easily adapted to these new markets although they all necessitated significant cultural change to satisfy different and disparate customer groups. Another example is of the company that was well versed in the mixing and blending of inorganic chemicals. Hitherto they had specialised in manufacturing products for the foundry market. One creative member was on a sightseeing visit to a deep mine and saw the miners mixing various chemicals to use in strata control. The visitor returned to his colleagues and passed on the idea that they could easily premix the mining requirements. A new business was born that spread to five continents.

The creative Champion needs to do attribute surveys of company product and then use his creative skills to hypothesise the application of these attributes to new prospective markets. The concept is seldom obvious, if it were someone would already have done it! The next stage is to look at the economic parameters and estimate the K!/K2 ROCE that prevail in that the prospective market and judge if we can add value. This is the concept stage.

Moving from concept to feasibility is a difficult process for of necessity the New Venturer has to draw in support from the corporation at many levels. Manufacturing, marketing, sales and finance all have to contribute to launch prototypes and to making bonds with new customer groups. Here we are forming ad hoc development teams. Commitment is now spread to much wider population, the disruption to routine is also now heavily onerous and this will generate considerable resistance.

These time fences in fig 8 are in themselves a very important discipline, however in harmony with all our other opposites, it is as well to note that many new ventures fail because they are abandoned too early, and many give ventures a bad name because they are abandoned too late. Once more a marriage of sound judgement and an emotional commitment form an abstract chemistry that makes the difference. Successful New Venture Champions are a rare breed because the courage to abandon or to fight on to continue, are both judgement calls, usually taken in a hostile environment.

The Job Description (much over simplified) for this appointment could be as follows: figure 11.

Job Title: Director of New Ventures.	**Reports to**: Main Board Director/CEO
Main purpose of job: To generate new ventures from corporate resources that will be practical and will lead to expanded and new market opportunities.	**Main relationships**: Main Board, heads of departments, own team (0-xx) Universities, Research centres, etc..
Budget: $ x	**Income**: $ y by year three
Key result areas	**Standards of Performance**
1 Present concepts to Board for approval.	1 At least one concept supported and funded in each period.(time fence)
2 Form effective development teams	2 Approved concepts reach feasibility stage by period (time fence)
3 At least one feasibility to market test each year	3 Market test results.(time fence)
4 Structure success market launches for hand over.	4 New venture consolidated into main business.

These alternate decisions both carry risk. Abandonment is an admission that the bird will not fly and to concede that the venture has been flawed. An ability to accept responsibility for a venture that has in the recent past, become a crusade, swallowed up development funds, caused untold interference in the day to day running of the enterprise, takes a considerable strength of character. It is important that should abandonment become necessary that leadership backs the decisions openly and continues to back other ventures that are in train.

Creativity is not a magic panacea for all ills, and creative innovation does not always succeed. One failure or one success do not define the process, a continual creative renewal is what characterises the 'creative corporation'. The use of intelligently structured creative development is not only a question of; 'what?' But also 'when?' Failures of timing are as frequent as failures of substance.

As new ventures frequently mean the introduction of new ideas to new markets, market acceptance, particularly in well established and traditional fields, often take years. The new entrant venturer can see the benefits of his/her idea but it may take an age to overcome the prejudices of the potential customer. These issues do not make the commitment to launch new ventures any easier. Clearly there is an aspect of the new venture process that has to accommodate this specific issue.

'If we have choices we must choose the route that is quickest to market balanced against the potential rewards'. K1/K2 never changes. We cannot wait for a traditional industry to overcome its prejudices against our new venture proposal even if we believe our idea to be the world's best. We have to retain our focus on keeping up our revenue in unit of time.

On the other hand if we are to produce the first self-ontained human living unit for use on Mars then our time frame will be longer; supported by shareholders with the belief in their long term reward.

The difference between long term 'Blue Sky' research and corporate new ventures is not clearly delineated. There is risk that those who see themselves in long term research ignore short term venture opportunity and there is also a great risk that corporate new ventures can be tempted into following impossible dreams.

There are challenges and choices here, certainly the K!/K2 is a useful model on which to build.

Hand on Heart:

- Do you have a New venture Champion?

- Is he/she the best person for the job?

- Does He/she have a job description?

- Does he/she have access across the Corporation?

Section 4

Creativity as a way of existence.

Let us imagine a corporation that embraced all the principles of continuous creativity, what would it be like? How different from the average of today? What would be the features that would stand out?

First, there is a clear and decisive leadership. That leadership understands the individually centred organisation with its inner, intermediate and outer ring relationships. The networks that exist flow freely and constructively through these ring relationships where hierarchical supervision is kept to a minimum. Supervisors and bosses exist primarily as delegators and facilitators.

There are fewer formal meetings and more informal task teams. There is a keen enthusiasm to learn from success and failures. There is a palpable and committed pursuit of customer satisfaction. There is a high degree of tolerance to achieving this goal. There is a system that everyone understands because initial training instilled that understanding and continual development reinforces it. There is respect for initiative at all levels and support for accountability associated with it.

There is a top to bottom awareness of corporate goals; these are frequently debated at all levels. Networks convey responses informally to the leadership. Leaders are happy to sit on desks or walk round factories to talk and to listen. They are not always accompanied by a hierarchical protocol.

Continuous improvements work through inner ring relations. Resultant actions are implemented through those networks, where resources are required supervision intercedes for budget support through formal proposals. Improvements to procedures not requiring budget support are formally proposed and acted upon through the networks.

Company performance is clearly understood by all employees, and progress reports published frequently. As many employees as is practical are encouraged to meet customers. Customers are encouraged to come and discuss their requirements not only with marketing but other functions that have any bearing on their product or service.

Individuals at all levels have regular job description reviews and appraisals with their supervisors.

There are regular training sessions to acquaint all staff with basic updating of skills including the creative skills. The Corporate culture map is updated and Human Resources wherever possible developed from within. Non performers are encouraged to leave. New employees are given emphatic familiarisation training particularly related to cultural aspect and expectations of the corporation.

The twin foundations of continuous improvement for survival and continuous creativity for rejuvenation have dissimilar resources but similar kudos.

All employees are encouraged to co-operate with new venture initiatives as additional tasks to those defined in their job descriptions.

The New Ventures Champion is well known across the corporation. He/she is a common sight in all departments.

This cryptic portrait on the creative enterprise I think encapsulates the key fundamentals, the twin foundations of improvement and creativity. In very large organisations the resources even at formative stages can be quite big. In a company like 3M, new venturing is a way of life where the whole corporation in deeply committed to new ideas and ways of doing things. I remember once visiting the 3M Head Quarters in Minnesota. I was there to see if our small enterprise could perhaps pick up a discarded idea that would suit our portfolio of developments. We were working on the upgrading of inorganic adhesives to see if we could get closer to the performance of organic polymers. I thought it was a low key visit. On arrival I was shown to a conference facility where I was amazed and rather overwhelmed to find a group of five new venture executive ready and eager to pick my brains. It was a shocking experience, for here was an organisation that really paid attention to new ventures in a very serious fashion. It was also frightening in the sense that the 3M guys were trying to pump me for ideas. I dumbed it down as best I could. I came away from the meeting having learned nothing of the 3M inorganic programme, I hoped I had given nothing away. What I did learn, was an insight as to why 3M was and remains such as innovative enterprise.

In a small propriety enterprise it may be the owner himself who drives the next generation of ideas, or at least, has a colleague who spends time on future developments and strategies.

In this book I have concentrated very narrowly on internally driven creative initiatives based on corporate strengths. I believe these initiatives are the ones most easily exploited and the most often ignored. For that reason the handbook exhorts you to examine the creative potential in expanding on existing attributes of existing processes, products and markets. It is clear however that there are other external sources of creative thrust.

A good creative Champion will use these external sources to augment existing knowledge and get exposure to views of corporate attributes from non-connected sources. Universities are an excellent source of stimuli and they generally give great value and insight into new opportunities that even the existing corporate leadership and those close to the business cannot see. It is important to remember that the university or any outside agency cannot and will not generate initiative within the corporation. This is not their job. They are there to learn and to sell their expertise.

Universities are becoming very much more aggressive about co-operation with industry and are increasingly keen to share the fruits of their labours by sharing patent rights and licensing agreements. Companies should be encouraged to live with this and welcome these fruitful partnerships. This does not imply an abdication from responsibility, rather the opposite; taking the commercial lead and creating new market realities. This does not exclude the use of academic institutions in a problem solving environment.

Hand on Heart:

- Are you looking for new ideas from within your known areas of strength?

- Are you reinforcing the creativity idea with regular training and forums throughout the company?

- Have you updated your culture map?

- Do you have contacts with Universities and learned Institutions?

Section 5

Recognise the difference.

Ideas are time sensitive, which is to say a good idea has a finite life span and that life span is often defined by events outside our control. Frequently several competitors seek to exploit the same root technology and we need to recognise that product or service improvements are not going to give us anything other than short term respite. Our regenerative creativity seeks to move beyond this phase and produce laterally stimulated ideas.

There is a difference between creative initiative and copying or developing from external existing factors such as competitor moves. These responses are in the continuous improvement area since the initiatives are based on existing data rather than new ideas. It is important that New Venture/Creative Champions are not diverted into these issues.

The extensive use of lateral thinking can be used as an adjunct, and a powerful tool in continuous improvement, and it should be used as a matter of course. This will come about if the skills of lateral thinking have been inculcated into the corporation as a tool and used in a range of problem solving activities. Nevertheless continuous improvement is centred on the existing body corporate; it's concerned with the short term responses that ensure survival and maintenance of the K1/K2 performance.

This is another example of opposites. We have argued that the new venture initiatives have to be integrated into operations at the prototype stage, yet here we argue that the Creative initiatives concerned with regeneration have to be kept separate. This can and does lead to conflict. For example there are time fences related to customer requirements that are inviolate and in corporations that find themselves in a constant catch up situation, it is clearly difficult for the New Venture Champion to command any resource at all. Incidentally the corporation playing constant catch up is probably passed its prime, and that makes the dedication of resources to regeneration all the more crucial.

Remedial action is most difficult in the climate of desperation. Nevertheless I hope that anyone who has read this hand book will have the courage even in the direst commercial stress to devote time and resources to creative regeneration. This may have to include dumping redundant assets and financing new resources for the creative initiative. Success is not guaranteed, but it will beat a slow and stressful commercial death. In short we have to exercise positive leadership even in crisis.

Hand on Heart:
- Is your latest idea really original or a copy? If the latter be prepared for a quick exit and enforced change.

- Do you have any original ideas under scrutiny?

- Are you making room, even in a tight ship, for New Venturing?

The White Book.

Making it happen.

Chapter1

Section 1

The Commitment.

Even if the corporation is up against it, as most of us are, then time and resources have to be dedicated to the nurturing of new ideas and embryonic new ventures. There is no room for compromise here. You are either in the business of internal regeneration or not. For most, this is too difficult and the attractions of buying extra market share too seductive; partnerships, mergers and acquisitions all intensely resource-hungry, consume not only resources but also destroy the cultures, particularly of the junior partner

White Book: **Rule 1. If we seek to regenerate from within our own, we will commit resources exclusively for this purpose.**

Rule 1 is difficult to apply in small corporations or private businesses that are already stretched, where the principal or one individual takes on this responsibility. It may be a part time job under these circumstances but it remains a permanent goal. Even when resources have to be shared; the goal has to be kept in mind and reviews of progress formally and regularly updated. So no matter how tough the going, however pinched the resources; the business of regeneration must have a place on the agenda and is never left to vegetate.

In the larger corporation the tendency for more negative bureaucratic behaviour is common. This is understandable; there are larger banks of assets, mountains of regulations to be observed, shareholders to keep satisfied and not least a large number of people to be trusted. Despite these complexities, creative change requires a loosening of the corporate reins. There are daily crises of one kind and another and just getting round the corporation is a daunting task. There is a vast corporate momentum, like a huge tanker ploughing the sea, the idea of a change of direction is an anathema.

In the larger corporation the energy and determination to pursue regeneration will survive if the responsibility is borne at the highest level. Persisting with our 'tanker' simile, the responsibility for regeneration has to be on the bridge, it cannot succeed from a humbler station. If the drive for regeneration is delegated to lower levels it will be swamped by the corporate momentum. **Rule 1,** therefore, has to be applied rigorously in small or large corporate structures. There is no difference between the two. In both cases those charged with the responsibility for regeneration have to have the absolute and committed support of the Principal or Chief Executive.

Whilst commitment has to start from the top, it goes without saying that the chances of success are immeasurably improved if the whole corporation shares the commitment. This seldom if ever happens. There are those who will always be unable to take their eyes off their own tasks and who will consider any diversion as an inconvenience, even worse, an idle and useless distraction. There are those who despite their valuable talents are not at ease with change or the uncertain. From these extremes there are a variety of attitudes that reflect the downside of the individually centred organisation; namely, that individual needs prevail. That this attitude is a denial of the network and inner ring relation principles is clear; however to some extent committed people need to have a devotion to their own key responsibilities and are bound to see distractions and change as threats, or at the very least, an unwanted complication.

Commitment from the top therefore has to mean more than just supporting the New Venture Champion; it requires relentless promotion of regeneration in good as well as bad times. This reinforcement of the 'Idea' as part of corporate philosophy must generate respect and attribute high value towards the regeneration principle and its practice. The involvement with 'new ventures' ought to carry with it a kudos and a prestige that implies a recognition that the corporate future rests in the hands of those involved and those who aid new venturing. This is a fast track to greater responsibility, a position of trust and the profitable deployment of our best minds.

Section 2

The Champion's lot.

We have agreed that we need to charge and entrust a leader with the task of regeneration and that is a continuous process that requires the commitment of the whole Body Corporate. We've already looked at a sample job description; fig.11, repeated here as a reminder.

Job Title: Director of New Ventures.	Reports to: Main Board Director/CEO
Main purpose of job: To generate new ventures from corporate resources that will be practical and will lead to expanded and new market opportunities.	Main Relationships: Main Board, Heads of Departments, R&D, own team (0-xx) Universities, Research Centres, etc
Budget: $ x	Income: $ y by year three
Key result areas	Standards of Performance
1 Present concepts to Board for approval.	1 At least one concept supported and funded in each period.(time fence)
2 Form effective development teams	2 Approved concepts reach feasibility stage by period (time fence)
3 At least one feasibility to market test each year	3 Market test results.(time fence)
4 Structure success market launches for hand over.	4 New venture consolidated into main business.

We've discussed the conditions in which the incumbent will have to survive, a complex of risk in the face of opposition, a need to drive change in the face of conflict and not least to learn to live with the strong possibility of failure through substance or timing. Not every ones idea of a comfortable job.

Comfortable it is not, this is a 'grit in the mill' situation, the job holder is constantly urging the consideration of new, often alarming ideas.

Why don't we try this?
This idea is interesting, shall we investigate it?
Why don't we look at remodelling our product and attacking a hitherto unknown market?
Can I spend money on a prototype unrelated to our present business?

These are not questions busy executives fighting today's battles want to hear. As we venture for the first time into new fields; the degree of scepticism is high, and opposition obdurate.

If there has been no internal systematic initiative towards the introduction of internal regeneration then even if we have a very committed and strong 'New Venture Champion' the chances are that he/she will be driven back into the woodwork never to be seen again. Or worse content himself with abstractions of no relevance, hiding away from conflict and dreaming dreams isolated, and apart from the mainstream.

We cannot start a culture change as dramatic as this without the most visible and enthusiastic support from the very top of the organisation. It is in this first tentative phase that most efforts fail, it's just too difficult to bring off without the right mix of Corporate Commitment that we've stated as rule 1.

Intelligent internal regeneration and creative development has to be allowed time to become ordinary rather than extraordinary. This is the Champion's role.

As well as delivering on the key result areas of the Job, (see fig 8.,) implicit in this role; the Champion is a major cultural influence in the business. Above all his other skills the Champion has to be a fluent communicator, articulating concepts, recruiting ad hoc support, persuading the Board to deliver development funds, and generating belief that is ventures are worth the extra mile of effort. The Champion manages at the edge as well as the centre.

The Champion has to have the discipline to respect the time fences that he's agreed. He must have a messianic zeal. The enthusiasm he generates that must be infectious and carry people along. Above all things the enthusiasm is the most important quality of all. The word enthusiasm derived from the Greek, means' the God within'; this inner indefatigable drive is a rare quality.

When ideas come as creative concepts it's often difficult to avoid the temptation to be diverted toward detailed assumptions, part of the first thought judgment even if we believe we have initially succeeded in suspended it. It is very important that the Champion learns to work firstly towards general principles arising from new ideas. The idea may well evolve into a related idea that is an improvement on the first idea. The point is that the Champion has not been diverted away from the original concept by details that will overwhelm the first idea before is has a chance to be developed. This is sometimes confused with 'Broad Brush Thinking' but this is not the case. In this case we are focusing on the new idea and empirically developing it without the hindrance of detail that is related to existing dominant ideas. Again we start with one thing at a time and in isolation, or rather, freedom from existing dominant ideas. This is a single mindedness that gives space and time to the idea to let it develop without encumbrance.

New ideas are not always good ones and are nothing until tested and proven. The Champion will certainly face the possibility that his idea; despite commitment and belief, will not work, cannot be improved and will not make the difference he supposed. This is the most difficult issue faced by anyone involved in New Venturing, to admit to the failure of the project. This needs confidence and courage a huge charge of emotional energy. As we've seen (see fig 10) all the more difficult to

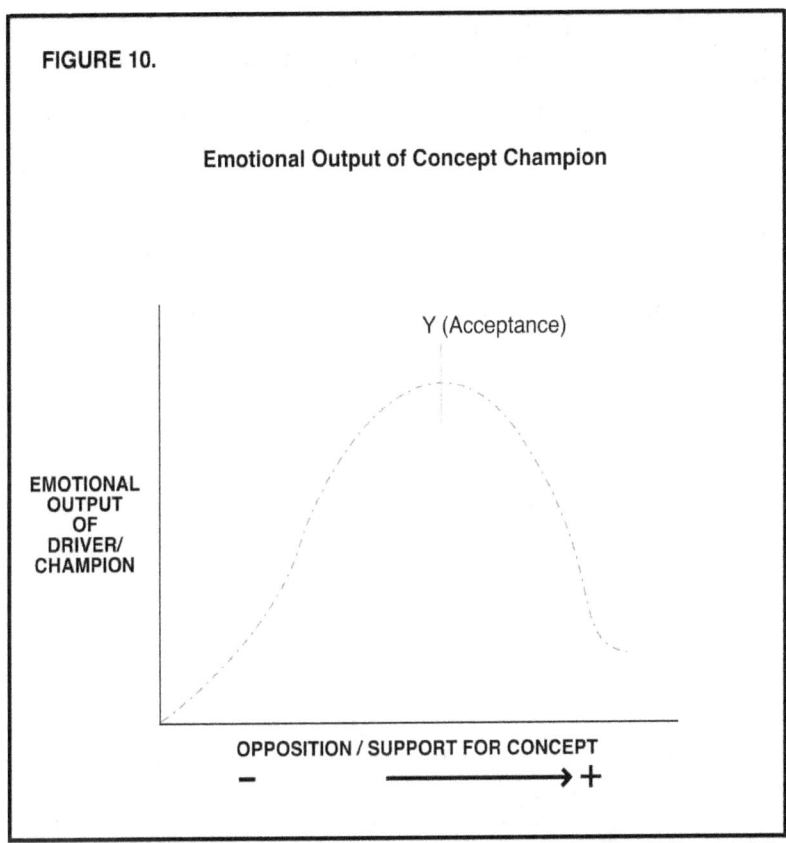

FIGURE 10.

Emotional Output of Concept Champion

Y (Acceptance)

EMOTIONAL
OUTPUT
OF
DRIVER/
CHAMPION

OPPOSITION / SUPPORT FOR CONCEPT

− ⟶ +

sustain without clear and articulate support of corporate leadership. Failure and the decision to pull out from a new venture is best announced by the Champion himself.

A profile is emerging here; I will use language not normally associated with 'business books' because I think it's appropriate. The people who make a difference to businesses have something more than their technical or entrepreneurial skills, they have interpersonal skills of a high order. We're talking words like 'gusto', 'joie de vivre', 'guts', 'imagination', 'fun', 'feisty', 'infectious enthusiasm', 'humour', 'care', 'inquisitiveness', 'integrity', as well as 'balls and brains'. No matter how mature or the past experience of the Champion; he must exercise real leadership skill.

Where do we find such a paragon? The best place to look is within the Corporation. There may be people there who are ideally suited to this cause. Often they are high performers who despite their undoubted talents are restless, lively and often described as a challenging to manage. They are often apparently impatient and take short cuts, but they deliver. If the organisation is viewed as an individually centred system this candidate will have a larger inner ring relationship or network than the average. This character is not a yes-man, indeed he/she is the very opposite.

The portfolio of experience required to do this job is as varied as the stars in the night sky. It's the ability to assimilate information and disseminate ideas in a language that is widely understood that are the core requirements. He/she will also be the sort of person who despite an apparent impatience, happily enjoys the company of others and listens to those who have vital knowledge. He/she will sometimes be seen not to suffer fools gladly, nor will he or she be seen as the best administrators on the planet but they will be orderly and have the tenacity to finish. Perhaps this combination of opposites; the ability to conceptualise, to drive ideas and to finish, is in the jargon of industrial psychology, a Shaper and a Completer Finisher.

If in your company, be it large or small, there may be good reason that you have to recruit for your Champion. How would we prepare the profile? Perhaps something like this:

1. Educational Benchmark Standard. (Unlikely to have been a research graduate.)
2. Data bank of experience. (Not too long in one discipline or business.)
3. Age (either under thirty with degree of innocence or over fifty with wide experience and a healthy scepticism and street credibility.)
4. An excellent communicator, verbal and written.
5. Strong personality with good network skills.
6. A sense of humour.
7. A Completer Finisher.
8. A potential CEO.
9. A grasp of the whole business theorem.

These kind of profiles are hard to find and even harder to judge. If the Corporation is forced to recruit from outside then the responsibility for the selection can only be that of the CEO or Proprietor. Consultants can certainly help in the trawling of potential candidates and administering the process, but this decision is a vital one and the cultural fit of candidate to the Corporation and his/her future influence can only be judged in house. There is no cop-out here. This appointment, whether it holds Board status or not, carries a huge amount of responsibility and influence on the future of the Corporation. The selection process must be rigorous with the final candidates under going interviews with a wide variety of the company leaders, and being asked to make presentations on their thoughts about the job. The CEO or proprietor will then chair the final selection panel.

This is a tough job. How long should the position be held by one individual? There are some who will relish the constant challenge, there are those who will want to take responsibility for a successful new venture and nurture it themselves. No matter what happens the job will never be redundant.

The White Book Rule 2 : Appoint a New Venture Leader who has the qualities of a Good Networker, Ambitious Completer Finisher, someone who whilst fitting in will have the courage and personality to lead change

Section 3

Rebuilding Rome.

Time remains our master, the clocks tick on. From the dawning of the idea, to the appointment of the New Venture Champion, to the first fruits of that policy lies a long and hard road. Commitment from the top is taken for granted, and hopefully, support will grow from within the organisation. Nevertheless once the idea of regeneration is promulgated there will be an expectation of results, of tangible benefits. There will be an element of scepticism and expectancy;" If you know a better way, show us." Will hang unspoken in the air.

Managing expectations is an important part of commitment and support. It is a march into unknown territory; there is no guarantee of success, especially in a short time scale. In a pharmaceutical corporation for example the decision to further research into a particular type of virus may be based on existing core strengths and track record i.e. an assumption that we are likely to have a good chance of success because of our track record, or it may be because that particular virus is spreading and creating a large demand for a cure, it has become a market imperative. Neither of these hypothetical drivers guarantees success, although both may be accepted as valid at the time of project instigation.

The research can be subject to time limits, though we could expect progress reports at predetermined intervals. We could set limits of resources, in terms of budgets, as well as time. Time can be relative though, as the reasons for our initial efforts are usually to respond to a demand; real or projected. If competitors beat us to a solution then we are clearly out of time. If fashions change and the perceived demand has changed, then again we've run out of time. If markets decline or become saturated then we are out of time, this goes for existing business as much as for new ventures. Our willingness to see things as they really are rather than what we would like them to be, is the key factor in the effectively managing expectations.

As time and money are invested into any project it becomes rather like a mounting I.O.U. The more time and money spent, the higher the required return. There has to be a time when the I.O.U. has to be called in, or it has to be forgiven. In the regeneration business we are further away from certainty than the pharmaceutical example above, for here we seek not a new product but a new direction and environment. Ideas are time dependent; they become outmoded not because they are bad ideas but because other ideas have made them redundant. Most things have stood the test of time because they work well enough, but this does not mean that there are not better ways, as yet undiscovered.

Regeneration and the search for new ideas do not take place in a static and passive environment. On the contrary they exist in the aggressive and rapidly changing theatre that is their raison d'etre. Commitment therefore has to be tempered with flexibility to recognise the ephemeral nature of validity of the idea, and have the both the patience to prove the hypotheses, as well as the courage to abandon it when it is overtaken by events. This is yet another conundrum of opposites that threads its way through our discourse and points to the probability of many false starts and abandoned hopes in the regenerative process.

If we start the regeneration process early enough, the pressure to rush through change for its own unqualified sake is lessened. Failures of embryonic new ventures are bound to bring traumatic stress; this can be lessened if we learn that these failures bring lessons of how to improve our next in initiative. Failures should however not be allowed to develop into a cynical rejection of the process but a redoubling of effort to find new beginnings.

Rule 3: There will be false starts and project failures. **Have patience to give these initiatives time, and a proper forum to test the result parameters. Encourage new starts.**

Section 4

Suspending Judgement.

Undoubtedly the most difficult behaviour change to facilitate regeneration is the ability to suspend judgement and allowing new ideas to see the light of day. All too often we dismiss new ideas with a less than cursory response. The natural reaction is all the more difficult to change. It is natural because the patterning systems in our thought processes imprint very strong and dominant ideas that dictate our first response or reflex thinking.

For example if you are a Brit you will know that it is proper in Britain to drive on the left side of the road. Likewise an American will know that it is proper to drive on the right side of the road. Both the American and the Brit will find it difficult to drive in each other's country despite the obvious demands to drive on the correct side of the road. The reflexes of each driver (first response reactions) will need to be consciously disciplined if an accident is to be avoided. This is made easier because their behaviour is heavily influenced by their new environment. They are in an artificial environment that makes it easier to change their reflex driving habits.

So it is with our first response thinking; we always revert to the dominant patterns that already exist in our minds and dismiss ideas that do not fit this dominant idea. Unless like the drivers referred to above we consciously discipline ourselves to suspend the dominant idea.

We've already seen that the culture of an organisation is the expression of the intellectual achievements of the social group; this is built from the reinforcing of certain dominant ideas that become 'corporate habit', manifested in certain expected and predefined behaviour.

When a group is presented with a new idea that is apparently out of sympathy with the Corporate dominant ideas, the new idea is naturally despatched with little thought or any analysis. We have said a number of times in this book, that it is very important to remember that the reason for the survival of ideas is simply that most ideas are not challenged. This is because they work well enough. There may be any number of ideas that will work better but they lie unused because the habit of using the original has become dominant by default.

This may sound a simple issue with an obvious solution; however it is hard to overestimate the barriers that individuals, and more so groups, put up against ideas that are not in sympathy with the accepted culture. Discontinuity or departure from the cultural idiom bring inevitable rebuttal. How does the organisation prepare itself to avoid these instinctive negative responses to new ideas?

White Book Rule 4: Establish a forum to listen and evaluate new ideas. This is developing the old and trusted method of brainstorming in a formal session; but the difference in this context is that the recipients or delegates to the forum are those who will be involved with the new idea and its evolution. Further they are given notice that the session is about listening without judging, and that supporting the delegates in this endeavour will be an artificial discipline that will ensure the idea is received by open minds. We are deliberately creating a mechanism that will encourage individuals to suspend judgement and escape from the dominant existing ideas.

There are many methods of doing this, all however give the idea Champion a formal platform to explain his or her idea and then to govern response mechanisms within tight artificial boundaries that detach the responses from the reflex reactions governed by the Corporate dominant ideas. De Bono's 'Six thinking Hats'[30], is a fine and very workable guide to such a system, there are others.

Each of these methods ensures an artificial and detached environment where thinking is structured in a predetermined way. In the new venture context the Champion may choose to elect that delegates are given notice of the ideas under discussion. These delegates are then invited to speak from one standpoint i.e.
What is good? then another delegate,
What we can grow from this idea?
What we can save from this idea?
How quickly could we develop this idea?
What ideas does this idea give rise to?
All these delegates are strictly confined within their boundaries. Note that none so far has been asked what is bad about the idea. Unusually the product Champion may perform this devil's advocate role.

The key issue here is that you cannot expect the body corporate or its individual members to respond to the extraordinary without removing the ordinary context. Detachment is vital if new ideas are to flourish, and only when they have been nurtured can they be re-attached to the routine. In so doing the change in corporate direction is integrated into the prevailing but changing culture.

---

[30] De Bono – Six Thinking Hats – Pelican Books

Section 5

Survival; from idea to embryo ventures.

The time during translation of an idea into an embryonic venture is the most difficult period; for the survival of new ventures is rare. Like most things they are most vulnerable at birth and in their earliest days. Under the pressures of the every day turmoil of survival and market battles the new venture is more of a nuisance than a boon; consuming as it must, resources and creating non-routine requirements from systems designed predominantly to do other things. The new venture can garner support from the enthusiastic trumpeting Champion, but time will swallow up that goodwill even in the most receptive of corporations.

Figure12 illustrates the relative pressure on new ventures; Supporters will put pressure on to get early results, whilst main stream struggling functions will see the department as a non-contributor and seek its closure. All these pressures will be conditioned by the prevailing health of the body corporate. When the corporate cycle is profitable and growing then there is no pressure to deliver or to economise, as the cycle peaks and declines then these pressures build. Sadly we often see the need to do something 'different' too late.

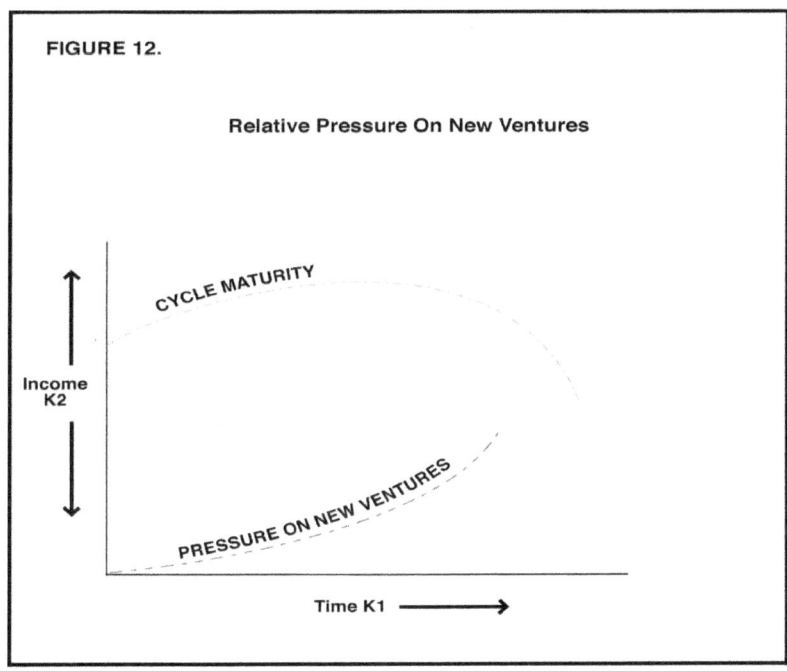

FIGURE 12.

Relative Pressure On New Ventures

CYCLE MATURITY

Income K2

PRESSURE ON NEW VENTURES

Time K1 ⟶

The degree of the intensity of defensive battle costs, the result of defending market share, will influence the pressure and ability to spare resources for the new venture. The steeper the curve of defensive cost the more pressure on the new venture cost. This is largely a consequence of the timing of the new venture initiative. It is obviously better to have new ventures in a contributing stage before defence costs become acute.

In many cases, the new venture regeneration idea has only been embraced because of fatigue pressure already prevalent. The down turn has been the motivation for change. Sad but true, this is more often the case than not. Here the pressures to slash and burn predominate, save costs and downsize is the order of the day. What chance, the new venture here?

Cooperation from every department will be hard to come by and even if people want to believe in the promises for the future, it's hard for them to drag themselves away from today's crisis.

Decisions on improving corporate results have to be made, down sizing of the core platform may be a must. **Rule 5: Even if you have to downsize: Protect new ventures.**

Section 6

Success can be dangerous.

It is a happy outcome if the new venture survives the pangs of birth, and signs begin to indicate a promising and potentially large contributor. Expectations begin to grow and the new venture takes on a starry lustre, attention is heaped upon it. Resources so recently denied are now more easily allocated and the new business member of the corporate family becomes the preferred choice for service.

Beware; for now the new venture will be eyed with envy by the Barons and the Masters of the old core enterprises. They will scent an excellent opportunity to ameliorate the damages of the defensive struggle. The new venture is doing well; what a place to deposit people and costs, it can afford it.

This is of course a recipe for disaster; for not only does the new venture become a convenient depository for costs and people, it also becomes the receptacle for old ways and old behaviour patterns. Old attitudes come to the fore, that insists on placing the old customer base, or process, or system up front. The new enterprise is soon submerged under the shadow of the old.

Racehorses do not pull carts, and that is an apt metaphor, remember it! The body Corporate and the new venture Champion have been through untold travails to launch a really promising new venture; they have all but succeeded in bringing about a significant regeneration that has probably taken at least two to three years of immense effort. Yet the scent of success has brought other predators driven by greed or jealousy, particularly in the larger enterprise. For example a senior executive is anxious to acquire new premises but does not have a strong case. He postulates the likely success of the new venture line, and builds the case for his new premises around it. The results will probably be terminal for the new venture that finds itself carrying enormous unplanned costs.

The error here is plain, risking too much in balance sheet items (fixed assets) depending on an untried new line. Had the company tested the new line first and not been carried away by the prospects of success then they would not have committed themselves to the new premises. This tendency to jump the gun in this illustration is not the fault of the new idea champion but the influence of others anxious to build an empire, improve status, whatever, clutching at the straw and using the new venture as a vehicle of convenience. "We'll need more room if the new line succeeds, won't we?" This implies tacit belief in the venture, and feeds the enthusiasm of the champion; it increases the support for the venture, alas, for all the wrong reasons.

An attractive new venture can be the centre for a turf war between the existing power brokers. The new venture, it will be argued, will fit well here, or here. No it won't. It has to have a large measure of autonomy if it is going to grow quickly, effectively, and become a force in its new sector or market.

This is not to say that the new venture should be allowed disproportionate resources, there should be the same discipline as for any other part of the business, but it must have a driver that reflects and reinforces the initial idea. If this is diluted then the venture is likely to loose its way and suffocate in the old culture.

There comes a time when the choice has to be made. Should the New venture Champion or one of his team be asked to head up the new business or should we draft in a new man to pick up the reigns? The new boss of this venture has to 'focus' (there; I've used the f word) and drive the enterprise forward developing its markets to growing K1/K2, espousing continuous improvement, eventually looking forward to incrementally develop the business with new creative energy within the relevant time.

When does a new venture come out of the nursery and get its own corporate identity depends on the size of the sponsoring parent. In a billion dollar enterprise the level of materiality will be much higher than in a small family business, but the rules are the same; as soon as the income K1 is material; i.e. when the business makes a discernable difference to period results.

Rule 6: Preserve the autonomy of the new venture.

Section 7

Time to say No!

From the acceptance of the initial concept of constant regeneration, the actual appointment of a new idea/venture Champion to an ultimate success is a long road. Sadly for some, it may be a long road, with no end. These failures to transform creative ideas into viable commercial entities are frequently caused by our failure to tolerate the demands that new ideas place on the organisation. It's not that the ideas themselves may be flawed; it's our ability to adapt that's most often at fault. That is not to say that all these created ideas are appropriate or timely, they are not. However filtering out ideas has never been a problem, it's quite the opposite, as we discussed in 'Suspending judgement'.

The question of proof is always an issue for the sceptic, and there are plenty of them in every organisation. In terms of new concepts or ideas there are no traditional methods of proof, only the parameters of success and failure derived from our hypotheses. Even in the most systematic attribute analysis of new markets or products there may be intractable problems. Unforeseen external events can overtake our initiatives; these may be from unseen competition, natural disasters, all manner of fashion changes or political forces. Often it is, that we are unable to convince the prospective customer that our new idea or product is of value. Often the new idea is ahead of its time.

K1 ticks on, our most valuable resource ebbs away. Our new venture has for what ever reason failed to live up to the promise and meet its goal within the time fences . Enthusiasm for the initiative may still be high; indeed most Champions worthy of the name are loath to give up on an idea that has consumed scarce resources and lakes of sweat. Part of the Champions role is to sell ideas and then to constantly reinforce the promise and earn time for the project to come to fruition. The problem as we've already seen illustrated in fig.12 is that the later that the project was started in the health cycle of the body corporate then the greater the pressure on the new venture, and the greater the likelihood that it will run out of time.

It is here that the committed Leadership either CEO or collective Board has to examine the original premise with the Champion. They must collectively agree that this or that venture be aborted or sustained. Time fences may be extended but this can be to procrastinate, that famous thief of time. Time and objectives have to be reviewed as a single issue, just giving more time for the same process can be right, but it does no harm to consistently review objectives in the same perspective.

Abortion is a nasty word, but the passing of time demands the decision to abandon or abort a new venture. The difficulty here is that many creative initiatives fail simply because they are ahead of their time. The champion may be an inspirational thinker who has indeed had a great and clever idea that really one day will revolutionise the market. On the other hand he may be a messianic egocentric individual who cannot let an idea go. (he may indeed be both: editor's timely note) In either case the

Champion will exert as much intellectual and emotional pressure as he or she can to prolong the life of his/her new brainchild.

Nevertheless and despite the pressures the plug has to be pulled, as negative costs pile up and the market shows little or no interest in the new idea or its consequences. And on this very issue, the idea or venture has to be judged, not only on its own hypothetical merit but also on the ability of the parent to sustain it. These matters are not nearly as clear cut as we might imagine. Very often a promising initiative can and does suck in enormous resources; there is greater and greater equity tied up. The idea of abandoning all those man hours and dollars becomes abhorrent, so we spend some more and so on. It is rather like a gambler doubling up on his bets.

This illustrates the vital nature of timing and the discipline of time fences and resource budgets in judging the progress of new ventures. Too early and we waste a good idea, too late and we may loose the company.

In a larger corporation there will probably a number of new initiatives or ventures in train; maybe a department of new venture executives are at work, each vying for his/her proposal to get the inside track. In this case abandonment is much easier. There are options to move to; "OK that seems a disappointment; let's move with more effort into the alternative." In the smaller operation there may be no such luxury.

Rule 7 Review new ventures according to predetermined time fences and budgets. Do not fudge, better to abandon early than too late.

Section 8

If you don't at first succeed.

In section 3 we stated that if a new idea fails it's not all that traumatic as far as the business is concerned, though it may be disastrous for the initiator of that idea. In section 7 we talked about abandoning new ventures where the consequences can indeed be traumatic. Dangers abound; it is potentially more dangerous if we abandon too late, rather than too early.

Importantly we have seen that the bigger corporation has a comfort level in its regeneration business because it is likely to be able to run with more than one new venture at a time.

The degree of trauma on encountering failure will be proportional to the expectation of the corporate need, and of course to the resource loss accumulated. It is easy to see that the abandonment of a project can turn the whole corporation off the idea of internal regeneration. The arguments for buying market share and relying on acquisitions come flooding back; surely buying existing business is less risky than creating brand new ventures. We won't repeat the arguments, there are plenty of the usual culprits to do it for us.

However no matter what the size of our company; if we have a formal expectation and structure to process creative thinking, we will have generated a number of ideas, many of them will be perceived to be better than others, a pecking order is established. The smaller corporation may only have the resources to exploit one idea at a time but there should be a forum to keep the regeneration ideas flowing and a constant revision of the 'bright idea' pecking order. We're building a pressure vessel of new ideas bursting to come out, and no matter how small the enterprise that is a very positive momentum; it's a great habit to encourage, to enjoy living in an exciting culture.

If this culture prevails when new ventures have to be abandoned then there is an enthusiasm to try again. The ideas will not be in short supply nor will the enthusiasm to exploit them.

Rule 8: Failure does not lessen the commitment. Try again!

Section 9

Repeating the Paradox.

At the beginning of this book I was adamant that one of the greatest threats to success was that we tend to repeat success formulae in changing circumstances and consequently get overtaken by events. Yet here we are close to the end of our discourse exhorting the readership that if you don't succeed try and try again.

Repeat the regeneration formula even if it has failed. The belief in our ability to regenerate from within our own resources is a commitment to perpetual change, improvement and renewal.

However that does not excuse us from closing the loop and applying our continuous improvement philosophy to the mechanics of regeneration. Failure as we have already made clear is less often due to the 'new idea'; failure is more likely to result from the application and execution of that idea. Frequently it is a question of timing, moving too quickly and expecting too much; or moving too slowly and loosing impetus and support.

We must also remember the pressure under which regeneration is usually practised. In a perfect world the time pressure to bring in a contributor would be relaxed. However in most cases there's an almost daily anticipation of success. Timing therefore is the single most important factor, many ideas fail because they remain incomplete, abandoned before they are translated into effective ventures. It is often a question of degree rather that substance. Expectations have been badly managed and the venture killed off prematurely.

An idea may be good, but it can prove to be too big for a small company. It is here that partnerships should be constructive and positive, marrying the resources of one partner with the ideas of the other. Beware the belief that the resource partner is the more powerful and ascendant. Respecting the 'ideas' partner as an equal is the only way to long term productive co-operation. The merging of two complementary skills, the functional and the creative, should be a union of equals.

Often there is an impatient expectation allowing the enthusiasm of the champion to run away with the venture. He becomes too cavalier and looses sight of the disciplines of time fences, goals and budgets.

Autonomy is often breached and the Robber Barons feed on the new venture too early in its life. It becomes swamped. It's not the piracy that's questioned it's the efficacy of the new venture itself.

Review the ventures that have not met expectations, and learn from them. There are factors that are common to them all:

1. Was the idea appropriately managed? Was the creative innovation incremental to existing operations? (It's of little use hypothesising about supersonic aircraft if we're in the scooter business.)

2. Is the Champion the right person?

3. Was the champion's role agreed and understood?

4. Was the external competitive environment well enough researched and understood?

5. Were the expectations reasonable, and were they reviewed within agreed time scales? Did we manage them well?

6. Did we devote enough resources to the project? Could we afford the necessary support? (Should we have sought an external partner?)

7. Did we allow the new venture the time and space to grow?

8. Did we pull out at the right time?

Rule 9: Continuously review and improve creative techniques and new venture Management

Section 10

Apply the rules.

Rule 1:. If we seek to regenerate from within our own, we will commit resources exclusively for this purpose. p.90

Rule 2 : Appoint a New Venture Leader who has the qualities of a Good Net worker, Ambitious Completer Finisher, someone who whilst fitting in will have the courage and personality to lead change. p.95

Rule 3: Have patience to give these initiatives time, and a proper forum to test the result parameters. Encourage new starts. p.97

Rule 4: Institutionalise a forum to listen and evaluate new ideas. p.98

Rule 5: Even if you have to downsize; protect New Ventures. p.100

Rule 6: Preserve the autonomy of the New Venture. p.102

Rule7: Review New Ventures according to predetermined time fences and budgets. Do not fudge, better to abandon early than too late. p.104

Rule 8: Failure does not lessen the commitment. Try again! p.105

Rule 9: Continually review and improve New Venture management. p.107

Rule 10: Apply rules 1 – 9.

Chapter 2

Making it work.

Fig 13 sums up the idea of corporate regeneration. Whatever the stage or size of your corporation be it small or large I believe that the ideas propounded in this hand book can help lengthen the life and health of it.

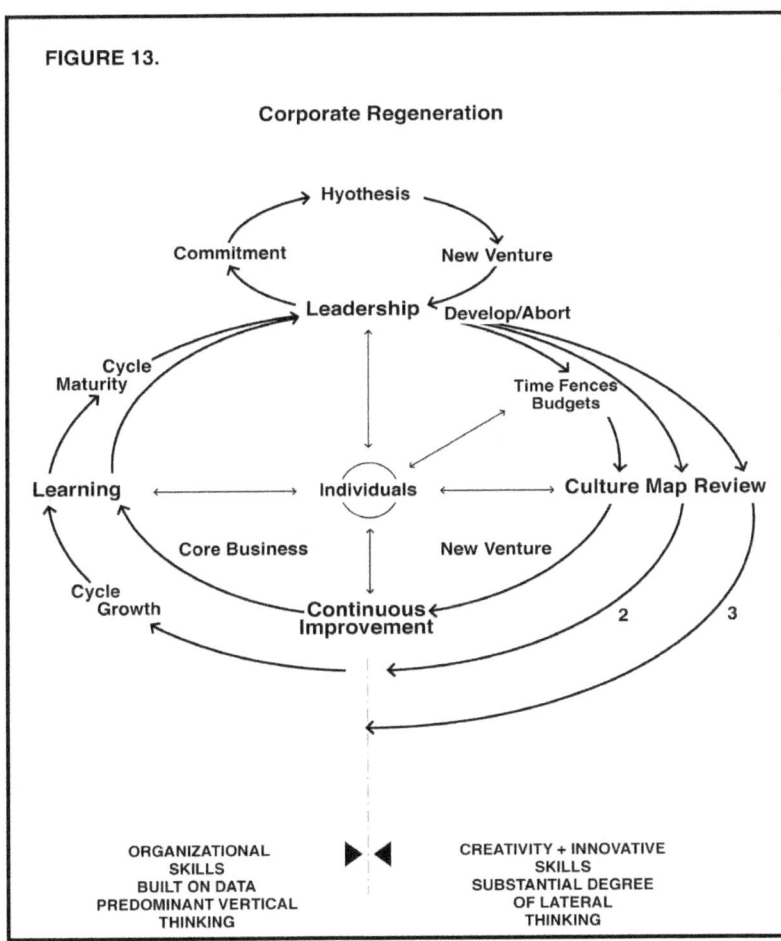

FIGURE 13.

Corporate Regeneration

There are two sides to every successful enterprise and they are in contrast and conflict for much of the time. These are the organisational and creative skills sets that rely largely on different methods of thinking. Both are vital to the health and regenerative ability of the body corporate.

We can call this left and right side thinking, or today and tomorrow; it doesn't really matter. That they both exist side by side is the key issue. Momentums of huge corporations tend to lead us to believe that there is no need for these contrasting styles to co-exist. In most cases today's success does not guarantee tomorrow's.

If we harness the conflicts that exist in these two opposites and recognise the virtue of each we can create a company where winning becomes a habit. The purpose of all this is to give that group of individuals we call the body corporate a chance of belonging to vibrant and lasting enterprises.

Bibliography:

Sir John Harvey Jones – Making it happen – Profile Books
Gary Hamel - Leading the revolution —Harvard Business School Press -2000
Edgar Schien – OrganisationalCulure & Leadership - Paperback
Peter Drucker's - The elements of decision making; The effective Executive Culture Shift - Price
Pritchett – Pritchett & Associates Inc.
Peter Drucker – The effective Executive- Harper Business
Michael Brassard – The Memory Jogger 11 – Goal/QPC
Bernard Burns – Managing Change – Prentice Hall
Bill George – Authentic Leadership – Jossy Bass Wiley
de Bono – Lateral Thinking for Managers – Mc Graw-Hill
R Max Wideman - Project & Program Management – Project Management Institute
Cameron & Quinn - Diagnosing & changing organizational culture
Blanchard & Johnson –The One Minute Manager – Berkley Books
John P Kotter – Leading Change
Getz & Drosdeck – Empowering Innovative People – Chicago:Probus Publ. Co..
Price Pratchett – Culture Shift
Donald Sull – Revival of the fittest
Sydney Finklestein – Why Smart Executives fail.
Hersham –The Key to Genius: Manic depression and the creative life – Prometheus 1988
de Bono – Lateral thinking for Managers – McGraw-Hill
Birch & Clegg – Imagination Engineering –(Challenging assumptions)
John J Kao - Managing Creativity – Prentice Hall 1991
De Bono – Six Thinking Hats – Pelican Books
Michael Michaelko – Cracking Creativity – Ten Speed Press 1998
Parnes Noller & Biondi – Guide to Creative Action- Scribner

www.ingramcontent.com/pod-product-compliance
Lightning Source LLC
Chambersburg PA
CBHW071837200526
45169CB00020B/1743